MERCEDES-BENZ

PRODUCTION MODELS • 1946-1975

**Detailed descriptions, specifications, photos,
production data and prices of all
1946-75 passenger automobiles**

With specification details of 1976 and 1977 models

by W. Robert Nitske

World-wide Distributors:
MOTORBOOKS INTERNATIONAL
Osceola, Wisconsin 54020 USA

Books by W. Robert Nitske

The Complete Mercedes Story (Macmillan, New York, 1955)

The Amazing Porsche and Volkswagen Story (Comet Press, New York, 1958)

Rudolf Diesel, Pioneer of the Age of Power (with Charles Wilson) (University of Oklahoma Press, Norman, 1965)

The Life of Wilhelm Conrad Röntgen, Discoverer of the X-Ray (University of Arizona Press, Tucson, 1971)

Travels in North America, 1822-1824 (translation of exploration diary of Duke Paul Wilhelm of Württemberg) (University of Oklahoma Press, Norman, 1973)

Mercedes-Benz 300 SL (Motorbooks International, Minneapolis, 1974)

The Zeppelin Story (A. S. Barnes & Company, Cranbury, 1977)

First Printing

*All illustrations are from the archives of
Daimler-Benz A.G.*

Designed by Ad/Graphics, Inc.
Printed by Shandling Lithographing Co., Inc.
Tucson, Arizona 85705

Library of Congress Cataloging in Publication Data
Nitske, W. Robert
Mercedes-Benz production models, 1946-1975.

1. Mercedes automobile. I. Title.
TL215.M4N518   629.22'22   77-8354
ISBN 0-87938-047-0

World-wide distributors:

Motorbooks International
Osceola, Wisconsin, U.S.A.

Table of Contents

Acknowledgements

Without the assistance of many fine people in the Daimler-Benz organization here and in Germany, these compilations of production details would, of course, have been impossible. I wish to express my most sincere thanks for all of the valuable help I received from Untertürkheim and Montvale, and especially to Herrn Claus-Peter Schulze in the Archives department and Frau Ruth Witzel in the Press-Photo section.

The final responsibility of the entire contents of this book is mine alone, however, and any seeming variations in the many detailed specifications, either inch or metric, are due often to the several documents used which did not always agree on every given model. Generally then, I have used what I felt was the most authoritative information available.

Production Eras

It is appropriate to begin this book on Mercedes Models with the year 1946. That year marked the beginning of the post-war production period and the Nallinger era, followed in 1963 by the Scherenberg era.

In the long and distinguished history of Daimler and Benz, there was always a definite engineering direction in their products, reflecting the personality of its then current Chef-Konstrukteur. It all began in 1900 when Wilhelm Maybach created the "New Daimler," developed from the 28-horsepower Phönix model built under the direction of Gottlieb Daimler in 1899. With the resounding success of this new 35-horsepower machine in Nice, the "Mercedes" era was first introduced.

Daimler received his basic patent number 28,022 for the fast-turning light gasoline engine on December 16, 1883. In October of that year, Karl Benz had established his Gas Engine Factory in Mannheim to build engines according to his own design.

On August 29, 1885, Daimler received patent number 36,423 for his vehicle and on January 29, 1886, Benz received patent number 37,435 from the Kaiserliche Patentamt for his motorwagon.

Wilhelm Maybach remained with Daimler until 1907 and was the creator of the powerful Mercedes racing car which in 1903 developed as much as 90 horsepower and in 1906 an astounding 120 horsepower.

Paul Daimler took over the responsibility of the Chief Constructor in 1907 to stay with the company until 1922. He made his debut with the 140-horsepower racing cars which astonished the automotive world with the decisive victories in the prestigious French Grand Prix. In 1910 the Knight patents for their engines was used, culminating in the 16/50-horsepower four-cylinder automobile in 1916 with that engine construction and a shaft drive, first used in 1905.

The 1914 racing cars — again to confound all expert observers — beat all competitors in the French Grand Prix. But Daimler's best remembered models were those using a supercharger. The 1921 models of 1.5 liter (6/25/40 horsepower) and 2.6 liter (10/40/65 horsepower) and the 2.0-liter racing car of 125 horsepower were truly exciting machines.

Ferdinand Porsche took over the leadership of the construction bureau in 1923 and remained there for five years. He was quick to capitalize on the victorious supercharged model and developed the four-cylinder engine into the six- and eight-cylinder types. In 1923 and 1924 the 2-, 4-, and 6-liter engines were used in passenger cars; and in 1928 the 2.6-, 3.5-, and 4.6-liter six- and eight-cylinder engines were used without superchargers in the sedan models Stuttgart, Mannheim, and Nürnberg.

In 1924 it was decided to merge the interests of the Daimler and the Benz companies and to create a unified construction bureau.

As usual, however, the best-remembered Porsche creations were the powerful supercharged sports cars. Beginning with the K-model in 1927, with a 6.2-liter engine of 24/100/140 horsepower, and the S model with the 6.8-liter engine developing 26/120/180 horsepower, these six-cylinder cars were further developed to appear in 1928 as the 7.1-liter 170/225 horsepower touring models SS and SSK.

In 1929 Hans Nibel took over the position of Chief Construction Engineer of the recently formed Daimler-

Benz Vis-à-Vis 1894

Daimler Vis-à-Vis 1894

Daimler Phoenix racer 1899

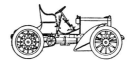

Mercedes racer 1901

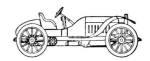

Mercedes racer 1906

Benz company. As early as 1908 he had startled everyone with his huge 200-horsepower Blitzen Benz, a fantastic car, which in 1909 established a world's record of 228.094 kilometers (141.7 miles) per hour in the United States to remain unbroken until 1924. With Max Wagner, Nibel was also responsible for the streamlined, rear-engined Benz Tropfenwagon of 1922. In the fall of 1926, Nibel joined the combined construction staff of the two merged firms, and was actively involved in the development details of the Porsche era models. (The SSK sports car of 1931 was a refinement of the touring car of 1928.)

In addition to the 1929 Nürnberg and Mannheim sedans, Nibel created the "Grosser Mercedes," a 7.7-liter limousine, with or without supercharger. A 1.7-liter six-cylinder sedan, the first car with swing axles, appeared in 1931, followed by similar 2-liter 200 models the following year. In 1934 the first rear-engined Mercedes, the 130 model, was built, and the 1.7-liter sedans using an X-shaped oval tubular chassis, 170V front-, and 170H rear-engined, attracted considerable comment. A 150H model followed soon.

Along with these many new construction models, Nibel also created in 1934 the first racing car for the 750-kilogram formula, the 3.3-liter 280-horsepower eight-cylinder machine; and from the eight-cylinder 380 model sports car with a supercharger of 1932 the 5-liter 100/160 horsepower 500K model sports car was developed.

After the sudden death of Nibel in 1934, Max Sailer — with Fritz Nallinger as deputy — took over the duties of the engineering division. Sailer, even more than most of his predecessors or successors, had been a successful racing competitor. In 1914 he had auspiciously participated in the French Grand Prix; in 1921 he won the Coppa Florio; and in 1923 he raced in the Memorial Day Classic at Indianapolis. He came to Untertürkheim from the position of

manager of the Marienfelde plant. During the Sailer era, the first diesel-engined passenger car was marketed in 1935 — the 260D with the 2.6-liter 45-horsepower engine, utilizing the pre-chamber combustion system patented by Prosper L'Orange and developed originally at Mannheim in 1923. The advent of this diesel-engined sedan opened up an entirely new aspect in passenger automobile power.

But the racing cars developed by Sailer attracted the greatest admiration of automobile enthusiasts. These were: (1) in 1935 the 4- to 5.6-liter eight-cylinder cars to develop 600 horsepower, (2) the victorious 3-liter twelve-cylinder racing cars for the 1938-1939 formula, and (3) the spectacular 1.5-liter car of 1939 with the two-stage supercharger. There was also the 5.6-liter twelve-cylinder record car in 1936.

In addition, the six-cylinder sedans of 3.2 liters, developed from the 2.9-liter engines of 1932, were brought out in a 3.4-liter version as model 320. The 5.4-liter 115/180 horsepower eight-cylinder sports model 540K of 1937 was a further development of the 500K of 1934. And, of course, the 7.7-liter 155/230 horsepower eight-cylinder supercharged engine appeared in 1937 in a vastly improved Grosser Mercedes, using an oval tubular frame. In 1938 the 230 sedan model had the first all-steel body.

Throughout this brief resume of automobile development at Daimler-Benz, considerable emphasis has been given to the construction of racing cars. They were a most important part of the construction activity, and the valuable experience gathered in strong competition added immensely to the technical progress in automotive evolution. Especially in Mercedes automobiles was the influence of racing and sports engines and chassis noticable, perhaps more than in the products of any other passenger car manufacturer.

Wilhelm Maybach began this episode with the 30/35-

4.5-l. Mercedes racer 1914

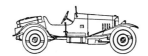
Mercedes sports-and racing car 1921

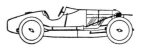
1.5-l. Mercedes sports-and racing car 1922

1.5-l. Mercedes racer 1923

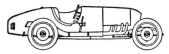
2-l Mercedes racer 1924

horsepower four-cylinder Mercedes of 1901 which two years later developed 60 and 90 horsepower and in 1905 an even 100 horsepower. In 1906 the huge six-cylinder engine developed 120 horsepower. The last Maybach racing car (1907) had only 80 horsepower, but with many improvements in construction the car actually outperformed the earlier models.

During the Paul Daimler era, Otto Schilling was especially concerned with the further development of racing car construction. The 130-horsepower Mercedes created tremendous admiration by the automotive public when in 1908 Christian Lautenschlager won the French race over twenty-three competitors at an average speed of 111.1 kilometers per hour and Otto Salzer drove the record lap at 126.5 kilometers (78.56 miles) per hour. The 1914 Mercedes made history by repeating the victorious feat. And the supercharged four-cylinder racing cars of 1921 and 1922 with the 1.5-, 2.6-, and 2-liter engines of 40, 65, and 125 horsepower were amazing machines, and way ahead of their times.

During the Ferdinand Porsche regime, the experience with the 2-liter eight-cylinder car of 1923 with supercharger led to that treatment for the 1914 model Grand Prix machines. The further developed 2-liter cars competed successfully in the Sicilian Targa and Coppa Florio, driven by Werner, Lautenschlager, and Neubauer. However, the construction of the fantastic sports models, K, S, SS, and SSK, with their huge 6- and 7-liter six-cylinder engines and whining superchargers are much better remembered by the general public.

But in 1934 Hans Nibel constructed for the new formula a racing car with an eight-cylinder engine of 3.3-liter displacement and 280 horsepower. Only twenty-eight years before the Maybach six-cylinder 11-liter engine (140 millimeter bore and 120 millimeter stroke) had developed 120 horsepower. (Prior to this time the S series of sports cars had participated in racing events during the difficult economic times of the post-war era.) The Nibel racing car engines had steel cylinders with four valves each with spark plugs located between them, and two overhead camshafts; the crankshaft had roller bearings. With this car the golden epoch of racing began for Mercedes. Rudolf Caracciola and this 750-kilogram car seemed invincible. The work of Hans Nibel remained in the capable hands of his assistants Max Sailer, Max Wagner, Albert Hees, and Fritz Nallinger.

Under the leadership of Max Sailer, the construction bureau developed the 4- and 5-liter eight-cylinder racing cars of 350 to 600 horsepower for the 1935-37 period along with a twelve-cylinder record car of 5.6-liters in 1936. Out of ten Grand Prix, Mercedes won nine events. In 1937, seven out of twelve Grandes Epreuves went to the Mercedes drivers. For the 1938 formula, the 3-liter twelve-cylinder racing car developing 450 horsepower was built. Even with less power the car reached the same average speeds of the earlier machines. Once again, the Mercedes drivers Caracciola, von Brauchitsch, and Lang were overwhelmingly successful in international competition — in fact so much so, that the Italians decided to allow only 1.5-liter cars in the prominent Tripoli race in 1939. Sailer and Wagner created, in record time and complete secrecy, the two-stage supercharged V-8 cylinder machine which gave Mercedes a double victory over twenty-eight other competitors. Lang averaged 197.8 kilometers (122.9 miles) per hour and Caracciola 191.9 km, a truly magnificent accomplishment of superb engineering and masterful driving of an excellent product.

The Fritz Nallinger era, officially begun late in 1940 after the Max Sailer reign, had its real beginning with the 170 gasoline vehicles of the Nibel period. Nallinger developed the 170V then to such a high level that it proved to

 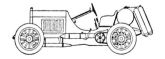 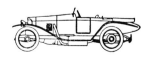 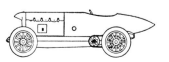 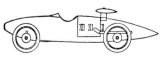

Benz racer 1900   Benz racer 1908   1.5-l. Benz sports car 1922   Blitzen Benz 1911   2-l. Benz Tropfen racer 1922

be the best-selling Mercedes model for ten years. The diesel engine was also further developed into the 1.76-liter unit by Max Wagner when Nallinger interruped his activity from the fall of 1945 to May 1948.

Since the various models constructed during this period will be presented in detail, it will be superfluous to summarize the Nallinger era in this section, except for a brief mention of the racing activities.

Greatly encouraged by the splendid successes with their 300SL sports car in international competition in 1952, Nallinger and his able assistants designed a new formula I car. The 196 made its debut in 1954 at the French Grand Prix with a startling double victory and won five Grands Prix that year and five in 1955, driven by Juan Manuel Fangio (eight), Karl Kling (one), and Sterling Moss (one). The 2.5-liter eight-cylinder engine of 76 millimeter bore and 68.8 millimeter stroke developed about 280 horsepower. A sports racing car, the 300SLR, based on the formula car, had a 3-liter engine of 300 horsepower at 7,500 rpm. It won the championship for Mercedes in 1955.

When Fritz Nallinger retired from his position in 1963, Hans Scherenberg took over the helm. The various models brought out at first were still those in the development stage of his predecessor, but the New Generation models showed the distinct imprint of the new head of the construction department and can unquestionably be considered as falling into the Scherenberg era. With the introduction in 1972 of the S-class of cars the change was complete.

One of the extra curricular constructions, the C-111, created much comment when first shown at the Frankfurt Auto Show in 1969. It was a highly sophisticated engineering exercise and a purely experimental car, but speculation — and hopes for the availability of such a vehicle to the buyer — ran high. The small coupe had a 3-chamber Wankel rotary engine of 1.8-liter displacement, developing 330 horsepower at 7,000 revolutions per minute. It reached 0-60 miles per hour in 4.9 seconds and had a maximum speed of 162 miles per hour. The rotary engine weighed only 275 pounds (against the 495 pounds of the V-8 of 230 horsepower) and had only 950 parts (the V-8 had 1,750). A year later, a 4-chamber rotary engine was installed and even better performance figures were achieved (0-60 in 4.7 seconds; maximum speed 186 mph). However, the Wankel rotary engine was not yet considered to be ready for installation in regular passenger cars.

The experimental C-111 was used in 1976 to establish several world speed records in slightly modified form with aerodynamic headlight fairing and solid wheel covers, and with a 5-cylinder diesel engine installed.

The basic power unit was that of the current 300D passenger car, but equipped with a Garrett Airesearch turbo charger. The engine developed over 200 horsepower at 4,200 to 4,700 revolutions per minute and had 275 ft/lb. (38 mkg) torque at 3,600 rpm. The final drive ratio in fifth gear was 2.7. The fastest average speed achieved was 158.368 miles per hour (254.856 kilometers per hour) for one hour. World records for 5,000 miles at 156.928 mph (252.540 kmph), for 10,000 kilometers at 156.748 mph (252.249 kmph), and for 10,000 miles at 156.467 mph (251.798 kmph), and thirteen class records were established in less than sixty-four hours of driving on the test track at Nardo, Italy, by four factory drivers/engineers (Moch, Liebold, Waxenberger, and Kadon). The event indicated the importance of this reliable, economical, and fast diesel engine and signified a trend to turbocharging of this well-established and still highly promising power plant by the imaginative Mercedes-Benz engineering department.

Another highly important project executed under the leadership of Hans Scherenberg, head of the Research and

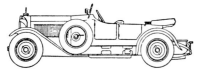
Mercedes-Benz Model K 1926

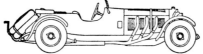
Mercedes-Benz Model S 1927

Mercedes-Benz Model SSK 1928

Mercedes-Benz Model SSKL 1931

Development Department, was the first of the special safety vehicles, the ESF (Experimentier-Sicherheits-Fahrzeug), constructed in 1971; even though passenger safety had always been a major consideration in the construction of Mercedes-Benz automobiles. This new safety vehicle included a vast number of outside and interior safety designs and devices and underwent extensive tests. Actually, more than a hundred safety elements had been developed and tested since 1946, and have been incorporated into the cars built. For instance, the cone type door lock was patented in 1949. In 1952 a patented body design, standard on all cars since 1959, was the safety body which upon impact would crush in front and rear but withstand exceptional forces in the extremely strong passenger compartment. Several ESF vehicles were built and exhaustively tested, and the ESF 24 looked startlingly similar to the production 450SE sedan.

Actually, the construction of safety cars was not new; in 1940 the experimental vehicle number 11 included the improved suspension system and such safety features as solid side protection and an extremely rigid floor and a three-part steering column. Design features over the years, adding to the safety of the cars built, were the complete independent wheel suspension in 1931, and the frame-floor construction and stressed chassis used since 1953. Engine features were the overhead camshaft design since 1952, the low-pivot single joint swing axle since 1954, power steering since 1959, air suspension system and automatic transmission since 1961, a dual circuit power braking with disc brakes for the entire passenger car line since 1963, a leveling adjustment device with coil springs available for all cars since 1965, the new diagonal-pivot swing axle from 1968 on, and electronic fuel injection since 1969. All of these advanced engineering designs made the cars safer to drive.

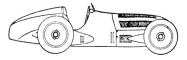
Mercedes-Benz racer 1936

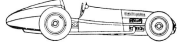
Mercedes-Benz racer 1938

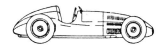
Mercedes-Benz racer 1939

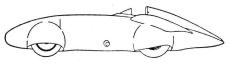
12-cyl. Mercedes-Benz record car 1936

From the dreary
wartime charcoal-
burning model (170) . . .

. . . to the handsome
small sedans of
more than thirty
years later.

1946-1975 Model Details

In April 1945, the directors of the Daimler-Benz A.G. issued a statement to the effect that the company had "for all practical purposes ceased to exist." The devastation of their manufacturing facilities was appalling. The Untertürkheim automobile factory complex was 70 percent destroyed and the Sindelfingen plant about 85 percent. The truck facilities at Mannheim were 20 percent destroyed and those at Gaggenau about 80 percent. What remained of the Berlin Marienfelde factory was dismantled and shipped off by the victors.

Fortunately, the Untertürkheim, Sindelfingen, and Mannheim plants were in the same military occupational zone and they could be effectively managed after as many former employees and workers as possible were located. The slow and tedious task of cleaning up the rubble was begun and the reconstruction of manufacturing facilities made some progress.

Vehicle production could only be accomplished if the manufacture of previous models would be continued. It was the natural choice of the directors to put the 170 model into production as soon as possible. The other models, the larger 230 or the massive 540K or even the prestigious 770, were of course, never considered for manufacture at this critical time in 1945.

At first, repair maintenance work on existing cars and some assembly of the L 3500 model commercial vehicles occupied the small working force and cleared facilities. The first post-war four-cylinder engine for a 170V model was completed February 22, 1946, but entire cars were not produced until June; a total of 214 units were manufactured that year. In 1947 it was 1,045 inits, and the following year production reached 5,116 units. By that time

the new currency reform had been instituted (on June 21, 1948) and the economy began to function properly. The financial paralysis ended with a sound governmental policy.

A Note on the U.S. Models

Prices quoted for the various models in the respective years are published merely as a matter of record. To compare those in Germany with their counterparts in the United States will only prove an exercise in frustration and drawing the obvious conclusions will be quite erroneous, at least for the models of recent years.

Because of the stricter emission and safety regulations, cars for the American market are equipped with many additional features. They also come furnished with many accessories generally available only optional at extra cost. For example, the United States 1976 price list enumerated 15 basic extra cost items for the 230 model and 6 for the 450SEL, while the German factory price list quoted actually 38 basic items for the 230.4 and 32 for the 450SEL as optional accessories. (A few were not available for U.S. cars.)

Nevertheless, despite the manifest futility, herewith are listed the exchange rates: In 1946 the U.S. dollar equalled about DM (German Mark) 2.50, but there was actually no official rate of exchange until 1948, when it was DM 3.33. In 1949 the rate was DM 4.20 which remained steady until 1961, when it was DM 3.98, and stayed that way until 1968. In 1969 the rate of exchange was DM 3.69, in 1970 DM 3.65, in 1971 DM 3.48, in 1972 DM 3.21, in 1973 DM 2.93, in 1974 DM 2.60, in 1975 DM 2.49, and in 1976 the average rate of exchange was DM 2.58. (Pitfalls here are that the rate varied, sometimes hugely, during a given year.)

Prices and Production

The 170V four-door sedan sold for . . . . .DM 6,200
    from July 1948. . . . . .DM 8,180
    from May 1949. . . . . .DM 7,800
    from January 1950 . . . . .DM 7,380
The 170Va four-door sedan sold for . . . . .DM 7,400
The 170Vb four-door sedan sold for . . . . .DM 7,900
In New York the 170 sedan sold for . . . .$ 2,850

Production of the 170V, 170Va, and 170Vb [Manufacturing designation 136 I-V] (from June 1946 until August 1953)

was in	1946	214 units
	1947	1,045 units
	1948	5,116 units
	1949	13,101 units
	1950	11,876 units
	1951	12,867 units
	1952	3,692 units
	1953	1,636 units
	total	49,367 units

Model 170V (1946-1953)

The four-cylinder engined 170V and 170H sedans had first been shown at the Berlin Auto Show in February 1936. Priced at 3,750 Reichsmark, this outstanding vehicle was thereafter available as a two-door and four-door sedan, open touring car, and even two- and four-door convertible, or cabriolet-limousine. And as a commercial vehicle, the 170 also came as an open or closed delivery van, ambulance, or police car.

The chassis was of oval tubes, and the three-bearing crankshaft engine was mounted on two rubber blocks for vibrationless operation. The independent rear suspension had coil springs, the front leaf springs. The chassis weighed 650 kilograms (1,433 pounds). With the 38-horsepower engine, the sedan reached a maximum speed of 100 kilometers (62 miles) per hour and used about 10 liters of fuel. By 1942 more than 90,000 units had been manufactured, providing impressive proof of the popularity of this model.

The 170V production in 1946 consisted almost exclusively of delivery trucks, ambulances, and police cruisers. In July 1947 the first passenger cars were assembled. This model remained practically unchanged until May 1950.

The 170Va, built from May 1950 until April 1952, had a larger engine (1.767 cubic centimeters) and greater horsepower (45), softer springing, telescope shock absorbers and larger brakes, as well as other improvements.

The 170Vb, built from May 1952 until September 1953, had a wider track, hypoid rear axle, a larger windshield and smoother hoodline.

Specifications

	170V	170Va / 170Vb
Engine type	4 cyl (M 136)	4 cyl (M 136)
Bore and Stroke	73.5 x 100mm (2.89 x 3.94 in)	75 x 100mm (2.95 x 3.94 in)
Displacement	1697 cc	1767 cc
Power output	38 hp (DIN) @ 3600 rpm	45 hp (DIN) @ 3600 rpm
Compression ratio	6:1 (from 1949: 6.5:1)	6.5:1
Torque	10 mkg @ 1800 rpm (72.35 ft/lb)	11 mkg @ 1800 rpm (79.59 ft/lb)
Carburetion	1 updraft carburetor Solex 30 BFLVS	
Engine speed at 100 km/hr	3300 rpm	3300 rpm
Gear ratios	I. 4.025:1 II. 2.280:1 III. 1.420:1 IV. 1.000:1	I. 4.025:1 II. 2.280:1 III. 1.420:1 IV. 1.000:1
Rear axle ratio	4.125:1	4.125:1
Chassis	X-shaped oval tubular	X-shaped oval tubular
Suspension	independent front, swing axle rear, with coil springs	
Brakes and area	drum, 564 cm^2 (87.4 sq in)	drum, 736 cm^2 (114 sq in)
Wheelbase	2845mm (112 in)	2845mm (112 in)
Track, front/rear	1310/1296mm (51.6/51.0 in)	Va: 1310/1342mm (51.6/52.8 in) Vb: 1310/1360mm (51.6/53.5 in)
Length	4285mm (168.7 in)	4285mm (168.7 in)
Width	1580mm (62.2 in)	1630mm (64.2 in)
Height	1610mm (63.4 in)	1610mm (63.4 in)
Ground clearance	185mm (7.3 in)	185mm (7.3 in)
Tires	5.50 x 16	5.50 x 16
Turning circle	11.5 meters (37.7 ft)	11.5 meters (37.7 ft)
Steering type and ratio	worm, 14.4:1	worm, 14.4:1
Weight	1160 kg (2552 lbs)	1185 kg (2607 lbs)
Maximum speed	108 km/hr (67 mph)	116 km/hr (72 mph)
Acceleration	36 sec 0-100 km	36 sec 0-100 km
Fuel consumption	11 liters/100 km (21 mpg)	10 liters (23.5 mpg)
Fuel tank capacity	42 liters (11.1 gallons)	42 liters (11.1 gallons)

Prices and Production

The 170S four-door sedan sold from 1949-1953 for. . . .DM 10,100
  convertible B, two-door sedan – 1949-1951 . . . . . . .DM 12,850
  convertible A, 2-3 seats coupe – 1949-1951 . . . . . . .DM 15,800

The 170S-V four-door sedan sold from 1953-1955 for . .DM 8,300

Production of the 170S [136 IV] (from May 1949 until February 1952)

was in	1949	3,370 units
	1950	14,735 units
	1951	10,333 units
	1952	326 units
	total	28,764 units

Production of the 170Sb [191] (from January 1952 until August 1953)

was in	1952	4,580 units
	1953	3,514 units
	total	8,094 units

Production of the 170S [136 IV] convertible (from May 1949 until November 1951)

was in	1949	39 units
	1950	1,686 units
	1951	708 units
	total	2,433 units

Production of the 170S-V [136 VIII] (from July 1953 until February 1955)

was in	1953	2,102 units
	1954	880 units
	1955	140 units
	total	3,122 units

Model 170S (1949-1955)

The 170S model, built from May 1949 to March 1952, was a further development of the V model sedan. The engine produced 52 horsepower. The valves were arranged side by side and a detachable light-alloy cylinder head was used. A downdraft Solex carburator was fitted with an air silencer and a wet-type air filter. The thermostat, set in the water circulation system, was so arranged that the heaviest work load in mountainous terrain would not cause any concern about water temperature. The drivability of the 170S showed a striking improvement, due to the more favorable weight distribution and center of gravity, with suitable track dimensions and the design of independent wheel suspension attached to the rigid cruciform frame of oval tube sections. Maximum speed was 120 kilometers (75 miles) per hour for this model which now had the larger body of the pre-war 230 model.

A convertible 170 model A was produced from May 1949 until February 1952, as was the model B, a convertible sedan.

The 170Sb, built from January 1952 until August 1953, had the gear shift lever attached to the steering wheel column, improved heating system, hypoid rear axle, wider track, and starting knob on the dashboard.

The 170S-V was to conclude the entire series. Built from July 1953 until February 1955, it incorporated the engine of the 170V, the chassis of the Sb with front axle of the V model, and the body of the S model.

Specifications

	170S / 170Sb	170S-V
Engine type	4 cyl (M 136)	4 cyl (M 136)
Bore and stroke	75 x 100mm (2.95 x 3.94 in)	75 x 100mm (2.95 x 3.94 in)
Displacement	1767 cc (107.7 cu in)	1767 cc (107.7 cu in)
Power output	52 hp (DIN) @ 4000 rpm	45 hp (DIN) @ 3600 rpm
Compression ratio	6.5:1	6.7:1
Torque	11.4 mkg @1800rpm (82.5 ft/lb)	11 mkg @ 1800 rpm (79.6 ft/lb)
Carburetion	1 downdraft carburetor Solex 32 PBJ	1 updraft carburetor Solex 30 BFLVS
Engine speed at 100 hm/hr	3330 rpm	3330 rpm
Gear ratio	I. 4.025:1 II. 2.280:1 III. 1.420:1 IV. 1.000:1	I. 4.025:1 II. 2.280:1 III. 1.420:1 IV. 1.000:1
Rear axle ratio	S: 4.375:1 Sb: 4.44:1	4.125:1
Chassis	X-shaped oval tubular	X-shaped oval tubular
Suspension	independent front, swing axle rear, with coil springs	
Brakes and area	drum, 736 cm² (114 sq in)	drum, 736 cm² (114 sq in)
Wheelbase	2845mm (112 in)	2845mm (112 in)
Track, front/rear	S: 1315/1420mm (51.57/55.89 in) Sb: 1315/1435mm (51.57/56.49 in)	1310/1435mm (51.6/56.5 in)
Length	4455mm (175.4 in)	4450mm (175.2 in)
Width	1684mm (66.3 in)	1685mm (66.3 in)
Height	1610mm (63.4 in)	1590mm (62.6 in)
Ground clearance	185mm (7.3 in)	185mm (7.3 in)
Tires	6.40 x 15	5.50 x 16
Turning circle	12 meters (39.37 ft)	12 meters (39.37 ft)
Steering type and ratio	worm, 13.9:1	worm, 14.1:1
Weight	S: 1220 kg (2684 lbs) Sb: 1250 kg (2750 lbs)	1220 kg (2684 lbs)
Maximum speed	122 km/hr (76 mph)	115 km/hr (71 mph)
Acceleration	32 sec 0-100 km	39 sec 0-100 km
Fuel consumption	12 liters/100 km (19.5 mpg)	11.5 liters (20.4 mpg)
Fuel tank capacity	47 liters (12.4 gallons)	47 liters (12.4 gallons)

Prices and Production

The 170D four-door sedan sold from May 1949 for . . . .DM 9,200
    and from January 1950 for . . . . .DM 8,620
The 170Da four-door sedan sold for . . . . .DM 8,900
The 170Db four-door sedan also sold for . . . . .DM 8,900
The 170DS four-door sedan sold for . . . . .DM 10,985
The 170S-D four-door sedan sold for. . . . . .DM 9,350

Production of the 170D, 170Da, and 170Db [136 I-VI] (from May 1949 to October 1953)

was in	1949	907 units
	1950	5,609 units
	1951	14,622 units
	1952	8,115 units
	1953	4,570 units
	total	33,823 untis

Production of the 170DS [191] (from January 1952 until August 1953)

was in	1952	6,734 units
	1953	6,251 units
	total	12,985 units

Production of the 170 S-D [136 VIII] (from July 1953 until September 1955)

was in	1953	6,494 units
	1954	5,992 units
	1955	2,401 units
	total	14,887 units

Model 170D (1949-1955)

The introduction of the 170D in May 1949 indicated an increase in production facilities and further advancement in the passenger car program. This diesel-engined car was an even more economical automobile than the gasoline-powered model and was particularily well suited at that time of economic hardship in the country.

The experience gained in 1936 with the 2.6-liter diesel-engined passenger sedan (45 horsepower at 3,000 revolutions per minute) was utilized in the creation of this smaller displacement engine which had the good qualities and liveliness of a gasoline engine; in fact, in some respects was even superior. The pre-combustion chamber system engine developed 38 horsepower at 3,200 revolutions per minute. The torque curve was very steady over a wide range of engine speeds. Despite the unpleasant engine noise at idling speed, the exceptional qualities of this diesel model were readily recognized. Maximum speed was 100 kilometers (62 miles) per hour and climbing ability 29 percent in first gear. Fuel consumption was 6.4 liters for 100 kilometers of driving. And, as in all cars, the maximum speed was also the cruising speed of the vehicle.

Since there was no difference in the gasoline-engined 170 models and those equipped with the diesel engine, it was natural that the change-over in the two models coincided. The 170Da production was begun in May 1950, when the 170D model was discontinued, and ran until April 1952. At that time the 170Db appeared, to be built until October 1953.

The 170DS was built from January 1952 until August 1953 and the 170S-D from July 1953 until September 1955.

Specifications

	170D	170Da / 170Db	170DS	170S-D
Engine type	4 cyl diesel (OM 636)	4 cyl diesel (OM 636)	4 cyl diesel (OM 636)	4 cyl diesel (OM 636)
Bore and stroke	73.5 x 100mm (2.98 x 3.94 in)	75 x 100mm (2.95 x 3.94 in)	75 x 100mm (2.95 x 3.94 in)	75 x 100mm (2.95 x 3.94 in)
Displacement	1697 cc (103.5 cu in)	1767 cc (107.7 cu in)	1767 cc (107.7 cu in)	1767 cc (107.7 cu in)
Power output	38 hp (DIN) @ 3200 rpm	40 hp (DIN) @ 3200 rpm	40 hp (DIN) @ 3200 rpm	40 hp (DIN) @ 3200 rpm
Compression ratio	19:1	19:1	19:1	19:1
Torque	9.8 mkg @ 2000 rpm (70.9 ft/lb)	9.8 mkg @ 2000 rpm (70.9 ft/lb)	10.3 mkg @ 2000 rpm (74.5 ft/lb)	10.3 mkg @ 2000 rpm (74.5 ft/lb)
Carburetion	Bosch injection pump (pre-combustion chamber)		Bosch injection pump (pre-combustion chamber)	
Engine speed at 100 km/hr	3330 rpm	3330 rpm	3330 rpm	3330 rpm
Gear ratios	I. 4.025:1 II. 2.280:1 III. 1.420:1 IV. 1.000:1	I. 4.025:1 II. 2.280:1 III. 1.420:1 IV. 1.000:1	I. 4.025:1 II. 2.280:1 III. 1.420:1 IV. 1.000:1	I. 4.025:1 II. 2.280:1 III. 1.420:1 IV. 1.000:1
Rear axle ratio	4.125:1	4.125:1	4.125:1	4.125:1
Chassis	X-shaped oval tubular	X-shaped oval tubular	X-shaped oval tubular	X-shaped oval tubular
Suspension	independent front and rear swing axle with coil springs		independent front and rear swing axle with coil springs	
Brakes and area	drum, 564 cm² (87.4 sq in)	drum, 736 cm² (114 sq in)	drum, 736 cm² (114 sq in)	drum, 736 cm² (114 sq in)
Wheelbase	2845mm (112 in)	2845mm (112 in)	2845mm (112 in)	2845mm (112 in)
Track, front/rear	1310/1296mm (51.6/51.0in)	Da: 1310/1342mm (51.6/52.8 in) Db: 1310/1360mm (51.6/53.5 in)	1315/1435mm (51.6/56.5 in)	1310/1435mm (51.6/56.5 in)
Length	4285mm (168.7 in)	4285mm (168.7 in)	4455mm (175.4 in)	4450mm (175.2 in)
Width	1580mm (62.2 in)	1630mm (64.2 in)	1684mm (66.3 in)	1685mm (66.3 in)
Height	1610mm (63.4 in)	1616mm (63.4 in)	1610mm (63.4 in)	1590mm (62.6 in)
Ground clearance	185mm (7.3 in)	185mm (7.3 in)	185mm (7.3 in)	185mm (7.3 in)
Tires	5.50 x 16	5.50 x 16	5.50 x 16	5.50 x 16
Turning circle	11.5 meters (37.7 ft)	11.5 meters (37.7 ft)	12 meters (39.37 ft)	12 meters (39.37 ft)
Steering type and ratio	worm, 14.4:1	worm, 14.4:1	worm, 13.9:1	worm, 14.1:1
Weight	1250 kg (2750 lbs)	1250 kg (2750 lbs)	1275 kg (2805 lbs)	1300 kg (2860 lbs)
Maximum speed	100 km/hr (62 mph)	105 km/hr (65 mph)	105 km/hr (65 mph)	105 km/hr (65 mph)
Acceleration	58 sec 0-100 km	50 sec 0-100 km	56 sec 0-100 km	56 sec 0-100 km
Fuel consumption	7.5 liters/100 km (32 mpg)	7.5 liters/100 km (32 mpg)	8.5 liters/100 km (27.75 mpg)	8.5 liters/100 km (27.75 mpg)
Fuel tank capacity	37 liters (9.8 gallons)	37 liters (9.8 gallons)	47 liters (12.4 gallons)	47 liters (12.4 gallons)

Prices and Production

The 220 four-door sedan sold for . . . . .DM 11,925
The 220 two-door convertible sedan sold for . . . . . . .DM 15,160
The 220 2-3 seater convertible sold for . . . . .DM 18,860
The 220 2-3 seater coupe sold for. . . . . .DM 20,850
The 220a four-door sedan sold for (in 1954). . . . . . . .DM 12,500
The 220 convertible sedan or coupe sold for. . . . . . . .DM 21,500
    (The 1954 and 1955 models did not get the "a")

Production of the 220 [187] (from July 1951 to May 1954)

was in	1951	3,453 units
	1952	9,165 units
	1953	3,322 units
	1954	214 units
	total	16,154 units

Production of the 220 convertible models, B and A [187] (from July 1951 to August 1955)

was in	1951	368 units
	1952	1,178 units
	1953	403 units
	1954	259 units
	1955	152 units
	total	2,360 units

Production of the 220a model [180 I] (from March 1954 to April 1956)

was in	1954	4,178 units
	1955	19,348 units
	1956	2,411 units
	total	25,937 units

Model 220 (1951-1956)

The 220 sedan was introduced at the Frankfurt Auto Show in April 1951. Regular production began in July of that year. In appearance this model closely resembled the proven 170S model, but the headlights were mounted in the fenders and the interior furnishings were more elegant. The good road-holding, soft suspension, and road safety were technically refined and superior in this six-cylinder automobile. The 2.2-liter overhead camshaft engine developed 80 horsepower at 4,600 revolutions per minute. The extremely quiet running short stroke engine had a specially balanced crankshaft and long water jackets to the cylinder parting line. The fully synchronized gear box was provided with a gear shift lever on the steering column. Special tuning of the suspension and a certain resilience of the front wheel suspension in a horizontal direction improved the suspension and achieved exceptional road-holding characteristics. The power-to-weight ratio of 16.5 kilograms (36.4 pounds) per horsepower was a considerable improvement over the 22.9 kilograms (50.5 pounds) of the 170S.

The 220 achieved 0 to 100 kilometers per hour in just 21 seconds and had a maximum and cruising speed of 140 kilometers (87 miles) per hour. With its elegant lines and fine interior, especially in the convertible sedan and convertible coupe, the 220 combined the qualities of a comfortable family car with those of a lively sports model.

The 220 sedan models were built from July 1951 to May 1954 and the convertible sedan types (B and A) from July 1951 to August 1955. A coupe model became available in May 1954; from 1954 on it came equipped with a curved windshield.

An improved 220a sedan with the new style body and the 85-horsepower engine was built in 1954. Introduced in March and produced from July, the model was built until April 1956.

Specifications

	220	220a
Engine type	6 cyl overhead camshaft (M180)	6 cyl overhead camshaft (M 180)
Bore and stroke	80 x 72.8mm (3.15 x 2.87 in)	80 x 72.8mm (3.15 x 2.87 in)
Displacement	2195 cc (133.9 cu in)	2195 cc (133.9 cu in)
Power output	80 hp (DIN) @ 4850 rpm	85 hp (DIN) @ 4800 rpm (92 hp SAE)
Compression ratio	6.5:1	7.6:1
Torque	14.5 mkg @ 2500 rpm (104.9 ft/lb)	16 mkg @ 2400 rpm (116 ft/lb @ 2500 rpm)
Carburetion	1 dual downdraft carburetor Solex 30 PAAJ	1 dual downdraft carburetor Solex 32 PAATJ
Engine speed at 100 km/hr	3470 rpm	3470 rpm
Gear ratios	I. 3.68:1 II. 2.25:1 III. 1.42:1 IV. 1.00:1	I. 3.40:1 later 3.52 II. 2.32:1 III. 1.52:1 IV. 1.00:1
Rear axle ratio	4.44	4.11 (37:9) finally 4.10 (41:10)
Chassis	X-shaped oval tubular	unit frame and body
Suspension	independent front, swing axle rear, with coil springs	independent front, single swing axle rear, with coil springs
Brakes and area	drum, 736 cm² (114 sq in)	drum, 1064 cm² (164.9 sq in)
Wheelbase	2845mm (112 in)	2820mm (111 in) convertible: 2700mm (106 in)
Track, front/rear	1315/1435mm (51.6/56.5 in)	1430/1470mm (56.3/57.7 in)
Length	4507mm (177.4 in) convertible A:4538mm (178.7 in)	4715mm (185.6 in) convertible: 4670mm (183.9 in)
Width	1685mm (66.3 in)	1740mm (68.5 in) convertible: 1760mm (69.3 in)
Height	1610mm (63.4 in) convertible A:1560mm (61.4 in)	1560mm (61.42 in) convertible: 1530mm (60.2 in)
Ground clearance	185mm (7.3 in)	185mm (7.3 in)
Tires	6.40 x 15	6.70 x 13
Turning circle	12 meters (39.37 ft)	11.7 meters (38.39 ft) convertible:11.4 meters (37.4 ft)
Steering type and ratio	worm, 13.9:1 (2.75 turns)	recirculating ball, 21.4:1 (4 turns)
Weight	1350 kg (2970 lbs) convertible: 1440 kg (3168 lbs)	1300 kg (2860 lbs) convertible: 1300 kg (2860 lbs)
Maximum speed	141 km/hr (87.5 mph) convertible B:140 km/hr convertible A:145 km/hr	150 km/hr (93 mph) convertible: 155 km/hr
Acceleration	21 sec 0-100 km	19 sec 0-100 km
Fuel consumption	14 liters/100 km (16.75 mpg) convertible A&B: 14.5 liters	13.5 liters/100 km (17.4 mpg) convertible: 14 liters
Fuel tank capacity	65 liters (17.2 gallons)	64 liters (16.9 gallons)

Model 300 (1951-1962)

The 300 model was also introduced to the public at the 1951 Frankfurt Show. It signified the return to the old custom of producing a truly outstanding luxury limousine of utmost comfort and superb roadability, capable of sustained high speed. It had a maximum and cruising speed of 160 kilometers (100 miles) per hour. The six-passenger sedan, with conservative lines, had a six-cylinder 3-liter overhead camshaft engine developing 115 horsepower. The short stroke engine with a special valve arrangement and combustion chamber design and thermostatically controlled water circulation and oil temperature, was most durable and extremely quiet running. It had a seven-bearing crankshaft. The chassis incorporated all of the features of the 170S plus a number of additional refinements such as a new steering mechanism design, electrical control of the auxiliary rear suspension which was adjustable from the driver's seat according to the load carried, hypoid bevel final drive, and dynamically balanced wheels. The car represented the ultimate in safety and riding comfort.

The 300 sedan was built from November 1951 until March 1954. It was also available in cabriolet form (pre-series production in April 1951 with regular production from March 1952). The type 300b, built from March 1954 until August 1955, had a more powerful engine (125 horsepower) and large dimension brakes, but the same body style. The 300c had an automatic transmission, two compound carburetors, higher compression, and better axle ratio, and was built from September 1955 until July 1957. The cabriolet D was available until July 1956, when a special model with a wheelbase of 3,150 millimeters and overall length of 5,165 millimeters was built on individual order. Then followed the 300d with a slightly modernized body style and fuel injection engine. It was available until March 1962.

Prices

The 300 four-door sedan sold for . . . . .DM	19,900
The 300 four-door convertible sedan D sold for. . . . . .DM	23,700
The 300b four-door sedan sold for . . . . .DM	22,000
The 300b four-door convertible sedan D sold for. . . . .DM	24,700
The 300c four-door sedan sold for . . . . .DM	22,000
The 300c four-door sedan "Automatic" sold for . . . . .DM	23,500
The 300c four-door convertible sedan D sold for . . . . .DM	24,700
The 300c four-door "Automatic" convertible sedan sold for . . . . .DM	26,200
The 300c four-door limousine with longer wheelbase was available at an additional. . . . . .DM	3,000
The 300d four-door sedan hardtop sold for . . . . .DM (available on special order only)	27,000
The 300d four-door sedan, hardtop "Automatic" . . . . .DM	28,500
The price of the 300 sedan in the United States was. . . .$	6,980

Production

Production of the 300 and 300b sedans [186 II-III] (from November 1951 until August 1955)

was in	1951	47 units
	1952	2,659 units
	1953	1,776 units
	1954	1,185 units
	1955	547 units
	total	6,214 units

Production of the 300 and 300b convertible sedans [186 II-III] (from April 1951/March 1952 until July 1955)*

was in	1951	2 units
	1952	262 units
	1953	181 units
	1954	87 units
	1955	59 units
	total	591 units

Production of the 300c sedans [186 IV] (from September 1955 until June 1956)

was in	1955	330 units
	1956	885 units
	1957	217 units
	total	1,432 units

Production of the 300c convertible sedans [186 IV] (from September/December 1955 until June 1956)

was in	1955	3 units
	1956	48 units
	total	51 units

Production of the 300d sedans [189] (from August/November 1957 until March 1962)

was in	1957	144 units
	1958	1,165 units
	1959	607 units
	1960	581 units
	1961	535 units
	1962	45 units
	total	3,077 units

Production of the 300d convertible sedans [189] (from July 1958 until February 1962)

was in	1958	3 units
	1959	23 units
	1960	22 units
	1961	16 units
	1962	1 units
	total	65 units

*Note: *When two different months are given as production figures, as in* April 1951/March 1952, *the first indicates the pre-production and the second the start of regular series production of the model.*

Specifications

	300	300b	300c	300d
Engine type	6 cyl overhead camshaft (M 186)	6 cyl overhead camshaft (M 186)	6 cyl overhead camshaft (M 186)	6 cyl overhead camshaft (M 189)
Bore and stroke	85 x 88mm (3.35 x 3.46 in)	85 x 88mm (3.35 x 3.46 in)	85 x 88mm (3.35 x 3.46 in)	85 x 88mm (3.35 x 3.46 in)
Displacement	2996 cc (182.7 cu in)	2996 cc (182.7 cu in)	2996 cc (182.7 cu in)	2996 cc (182.7 cu in)
Power output	115 hp (DIN) @ 4600 rpm	125 hp (DIN) @ 4500 rpm (136 hp SAE)	125 hp (DIN) @ 4500 rpm (136 hp SAE)	160 hp (DIN) @ 5300 rpm (180 hp SAE)
Compression ratio	6.4:1	7.4-7.5:1	7.4-7.5:1	8.55:1
Torque	20 mkg @ 2500 rpm (114 ft/lb)	22.5 mkg @ 2600 rpm (163 ft/lb)	22.5 mkg @ 2600 rpm (163 ft/lb)	24.2 mkg @ 4200 rpm (175 ft/lb)
Carburetion	2 dual downdraft carburetors Solex 40 PBJC	2 dual downdraft carburetors Solex 32 PAJAT	2 dual downdraft carburetors	Bosch injection pump
Engine speed at 100 km/hr	3300 rpm	3300 rpm	3300 rpm (manual)	3300 rpm (automatic, 3-speed)
Gear ratios	I. 2.95:1 (later 3.30:1) II. 2.13:1 III. 1.46:1 IV. 1.00:1	I. 3.44:1 II. 2.30:1 III. 1.53:1 IV. 1.00:1	I. 3.44:1 II. 2.30:1 III. 1.53:1 IV. 1.00:1	I. 2.303:1 II. 1.435:1 III. 1.00:1
Rear axle ratio	4.44	4.67	4.67	4.67
Chassis	X-shaped oval tubular	X-shaped oval tubular	X-shaped oval tubular	X-shaped oval tubular
Suspension	independent front, swing axle rear, with coil springs		independent front, single swing axle rear, with coil springs	
Brakes and area	drum, 1270 cm² (197 sq in)	drum, 1470 cm² (228 sq in)	drum, 1470 cm² (227.9 sq in)	drum, 1470 cm² (227.9 sq in)
Wheelbase	3050mm (120 in)	3050mm (120 in)	3050mm (120 in)	3150mm (124 in)
Track, front/rear	1480/1525mm (58.2/60 in)	1480/1525mm (58.2/60 in)	1480/1525mm (58.3/60.0 in)	1480/1525mm (58.3/60.0 in)
Length	4950mm (194.9 in)	5065mm (199.4 in)	5065mm (199.4 in)	5190mm (204.3 in)
Width	1838mm (72.4 in)	1838 (72.4 in)	1838mm (72.4 in)	1860mm (73.2 in)
Height	1600mm (63.0 in)	1640mm (64.6 in)	1600mm (63.0 in)	1620mm (63.8 in)
Ground clearance	185mm (7.3 in)	185mm (7.3 in)	185mm (7.3 in)	185mm (7.3 in)
Tires	7.10 x 15 extra	7.10 x 15 extra	7.60 x 15 extra	7.60 x 15 extra
Turning circle	12.6-13.1 meters (41-43 ft)	12.6-13.1 meters (41-43 ft)	12.6-13.1 meters (41-43 ft)	12.8-13.3 meters (42-44 ft)
Steering type and ratio	worm, 17.9:1 (3.3 turns)	recirculating ball, 21.4:1 (3.75 turns)	recirculating ball, 21.4:1 (3.75 turns)	from Sept. '58 servo-assist, optional
Weight (automatic)	1780 kg (3916 lbs) convertible: 1830 kg (4026 lbs)		1860 kg (4092 lbs) convertible: 1910 kg (4202 lbs) 1910 kg (4202 lbs) convertible: 1960 kg (4312 lbs)	1950 kg (4290 lbs) 2000 kg (4400 lbs)
Maximum speed (automatic)	160 km/hr (99.5 mph)	163 km/hr (101 mph)	160 km/hr (99.5 mph) 155 km/hr (96.3 mph)	170 km/hr (105.6 mph) 165 km/hr (102.5 mph)
Acceleration (automatic)	18 sec 0-100 km	17 sec 0-100 km	17 sec 0-100 km 18 sec 0-100 km	17 sec 0-100 km 18 sec 0-100 km
Fuel consumption (automatic)	16.5 liters/100 km (14.2 mpg)	16 liters, super (14.7 mpg)	16 liters, super (14.7 mpg) 17 liters, super (13.7 mpg)	17 liters, super (13.7 mpg) 18 liters, super (13 mpg)
Fuel tank capacity	72 liters (19 gallons)	72 liters (19 gallons)	72 liters (19 gallons)	72 liters (19 gallons)

Prices and Production

The 300S coupe, convertible A, and roadster sold for DM 34,500. When in 1953 a new, modern showroom with excellent service facilities for Mercedes-Benz automobiles was opened at New York by the Hoffman Motor Company, importers for these cars in the United States, the 300S was priced at $12,500. The 300Sc coupe, convertible A, and open roadster sold for DM 36,500.

Production of the 300S model [188 I] (from September 1951/July 1952 until August 1955)

	was in 1951	2 units
	1952	113 units
	1953	353 units
	1954	37 units
	1955	55 units
	total	560 units

Production of the 300Sc model [188 II] (from September/December 1955 to April 1958)

	was in 1955	5 units
	1956	140 units
	1957	52 units
	1958	3 units
	total	200 units

Model 300S (1951-1958)

The 300S (super) model, first shown at the Paris Salon in October 1951 and produced in 1952, was created for the discriminating sports enthusiast driver. It was designed to carry on the tradition which had begun twenty-five years before with the 6-liter K model of 1927, followed by the superb S and SS models and finally the 540K model of 1936. With but half of the engine displacement, without supercharger, and weighing a ton less than its illustrious predecessor (and 450 pounds less than the 300 sedan), the 300S was actually faster, more responsive, safer, and more comfortable. (Karl Kling drove better times at the Nürburgring than with any other Mercedes since the SSK model.) The 540K had a 180-horsepower engine and weighed 5,735 pounds; the 300S had a 150 horsepower engine and weighed 3,880 pounds. Maximum speed was 109 miles per hour. The engine had a compression ratio of 7.5 to 1 and three downdraft carburetors. The wheelbase was 2,900 millimeters (114.2 inches) and overall length 4,700 millimeters (185 inches).

Two body styles were available, the coupe and convertible coupe or open roadster. The interior furnishings were of the finest material, real leather upholstery and rich wood matching the dash and the trim around the side and rear windows. The 300S was a joy to drive and to own, as this chronicler was fortunate to experience in ten years and a hundred thousand miles.

The 300Sc model was built from September 1955 until April 1958. That car had a fuel injection engine and single pivot swing axle, but was outwardly the same as the previous type, except that the rubber center piece in the bumpers was left off. A total of only 760 automobiles of both model types were produced.

Specifications

	300S	300Sc
Engine type	6 cyl overhead camshaft (M 188)	6 cyl overhead camshaft (M 188)
Bore stroke	85 x 88mm (3.35 x 3.46 in)	85 x 88mm (3.35 x 3.46 in)
Displacement	2996 cc (182.7 cu in)	2996 cc (182.7 cu in)
Power output	150 hp (DIN) @ 5000 rpm	175 hp (DIN) @ 5400 rpm
Compression ratio	7.8:1	8.55:1
Torque	23.5 mkg @ 3800 rpm (170 ft/lb)	26 mkg @ 4300 rpm 188 ft/lb)
Carburetion	3 downdraft carburetors Solex 40 PBJC	Bosch injection pump
Engine speed at 100 km/hr	3260 rpm	3260 rpm
Gear ratios	I. 3.33:1 (later 3.68:1) II. 2.12:1 (later 2.25:1) III. 1.46:1 (later 1.42:1) IV. 1.00:1 (later 1.00:1)	I. 3.55:1 II. 2.30:1 III. 1.53:1 IV. 1.00:1
Rear axle ratio	4.125	4.44
Chassis	X-shaped oval tubular frame	X-shaped oval tubular frame
Suspension	independent front, swing axle rear, with coil springs	independent front, single pivot swing axle rear, with coil springs
Brakes and area	drum, 1270 cm^2 (197 sq in)	drum, 1470 cm^2 (228 sq in)
Wheelbase	2900mm (114.2 in)	2900mm (114.2 in)
Track, front/rear	1480/1525mm (58.2/60 in)	1480/1525mm (58.2/60 in)
Length	4700mm (185 in)	4700mm (185 in)
Width	1860mm (73.2 in)	1860mm (73.2 in)
Height	1510mm (59.4 in)	1510mm (59.4 in)
Ground clearance	180mm (7.1 in)	180mm (7.1 in)
Tires	6.70 x 15 extra	6.70 x 15 extra
Turning circle	12.2-12.7 meters (40-42 ft)	12.2-12.7 meters (40-42 ft)
Steering type and ratio	recirculating ball, 21.4:1 (3.75 turns)	recirculating ball, 21.4:1 (3.75 turns)
Weight	1760 kg (3880 lbs)	1780 kg (3924 lbs)
Maximum speed	176 km/hr (109 mph)	180 km/hr (112 mph)
Acceleration	15 sec 0-100 km	14 sec 0-100 km
Fuel consumption	17 liters, super/100 km (13.7 mpg)	
Fuel tank capacity	85 liters (22 gallons)	85 liters (22 gallons)

Prices

The 180 four-door sedan sold in 1953-1954 for . . . . . .DM 9,950
   (The U.S. price was $3,350 on the West coast)
   in 1954-1956 . . . . .DM 9,450
   in 1956-1961 . . . . .DM 8,700
   from August 1961 . . . . .DM 8,950
   from April 1962 . . . . .DM 9,350

For 180b and 180c power-assisted brakes were available at DM 300 extra cost.

Model 180 (1953-1962)

The 180 model, introduced in early 1953, featured a radically new type of chassis design, although the x-shaped oval tubular frame, used on the previous models, had proven thoroughly satisfactory. The most important element in this new design was that high sectional steel side members were united to the floor of the body to make a platform, greatly resistant to distortion. It actually doubled the rigidity of the assembly and considerably lessened noise.

The subframe which carried the entire power unit and transmission, as well as the steering and front wheel assembly, was anchored to the front part of the main chassis on rubber blocks on the three-point suspension system. This arrangement offered advantages in manufacture and maintenance. It was also the first example of a design where heavy components were readily detachable.

The double-joint swing axle was retained; and so was the four-cylinder, 1,767 cubic centimeter, 52-horsepower engine of the 170S model because of its ready availability and proven reliability. The external lines of the rather stubby-looking 180 model were in keeping with modern tendencies but retained the traditional radiator style. The radiator shell lifted up with the hood. The car was 22 percent roomier and more comfortable, more economical to operate, and allowed the driver an excellent view of the road. The window area was 40 percent greater than that of the 170S model. The smooth running and ideal road-holding properties were such that the driver was hardly aware of having reached its maximum speed of 125 kilometers (78 miles) per hour. The 180 model was built from September 1953 until August 1957. The 180a, built from September 1957 until July 1959, had the larger engine, 1,897 cubic centimeters and 65 horsepower. The 180b followed until August 1961. It had larger brakes, wider radiator, and no vertical bars on the bumpers. The 180c, with a changed valve gear was built from June 1961 until October 1962.

Production

Production of the 180 model [120 I] (from July 1953 until June 1957)

was in	1953	4,362 units
	1954	20,306 units
	1955	17,704 units
	1956	8,464 units
	1957	1,350 units
	total	52,186 units

Production of the 180a model [120 II] from June 1957 until July 1959)

was in	1957	4,656 units
	1958	15,967 units
	1959	6,730 units
	total	27,353 units

Production of the 180b model [120 III] (from July 1959 until August 1961)

was in	1959	7,314 units
	1960	14,384 units
	1961	7,717 units
	total	29,415 units

Production of the 180c model [120 IV] (from June 1961 until October 1962)

was in	1961	4,980 units
	1962	4,300 units
	total	9,280 units

Specifications

	180	180a, b, c
Engine type	4 cyl (M 136)	4 cyl (M 136)
Bore and stroke	75 x 100mm (2.96 x 3.94 in)	85 x 83.6mm (3.35 x 3.29 in)
Displacement	1767 cc (107.7 cu in)	1897 cc (115.7 cu in)
Power output	52 hp (DIN) @ 4000 rpm	65 hp (DIN) @ 4500 rpm b: 68 hp (DIN) @ 4400 rpm
Compression ratio	6.8:1	6.8:1 b: 7:1
Torque	11.4 mkg @ 1800 rpm (82.5 ft/lb)	13 mkg @ 2200 rpm (94 ft/lb) b: 13.2 mkg @ 2500 rpm (96/4 ft/lb)
Carburetion	1 downdraft carburetor Solex 32 PICB	1 downdraft carburetor Solex 32 PICB b: Solex 34 PICB
Engine speed at 100 km/hr	3390 rpm	3390 rpm
Gear ratios	I. 4.05:1 II. 2.38:1 III. 1.53:1 IV. 1.00:1	I. 4.05:1 II. 2.38:1 III. 1.53:1 IV. 1.00:1
Rear axle ratio	3.89 (35:9)	3.90 (39:10)
Chassis	unit frame and body	unit frame and body
Suspension	independent front, swing axle rear, with coil springs from Sept '55: single swing axle	
Brakes and area	drum 816 cm^2 (126.5 sq in)	b: drum, 1064 cm^2 (164.9 sq in) servo optional
Wheelbase	2650mm (104.3 in)	2650mm (104.3 in)
Track, front/rear	1420/1475mm (55.9/58.1 in)	1420/1475mm (55.9/58.1 in)
Length	4480mm (176.4 in)	4480mm (176.4 in)
Width	1740mm (68.5 in)	1740mm (68.5 in)
Height	1560mm (61.4 in)	1560mm (61.4 in)
Ground clearance	185mm (7.3 in)	185mm (7.3 in)
Tires	6.40 x 13	6.40 x 13
Turning circle	11.5 meters (38 ft)	11.5 meters (38 ft)
Steering type and ratio	recirculating ball, 18.5:1	recirculating ball, 18.5:1
Weight	1180 kg (2596 lbs) from Sept: 1200 kg (2640 lbs)	1210 kg (2662 lbs)
Maximum speed	126 km/hr (78.4 mph)	136 km/hr (84 mph)
Acceleration	31 sec 0-100 km	21 sec 0-100 km
Fuel consumption	11.5 liters/100 km (20.4 mpg)	10.5 liters (22.4 mpg)
Fuel tank capacity	56 liters (14.8 gallons)	56 liters (14.8 gallons)

Prices and Production

The 180D four-door sedan sold in 1954-1955 for . . . . .DM 10,300
   in 1956 . . . . .DM 9,850
   in 1956-1958 . . . . .DM 9,480
   in 1958-1961 . . . . .DM 9,200
   from August 1961 . . . . .DM 9,450
   from April 1962 . . . . .DM 9,850

Production of the 180D model [120 I] (from October 1953/
February 1954 until July 1959)

was in	1953	11 units
	1954	15,532 units
	1955	20,345 units
	1956	21,013 units
	1957	22,910 units
	1958	26,693 units
	1959	9,981 units
total	116,485 units	

Production of the 180Db [120 II] (from July 1959 until August
1961)

was in	1959	8,076 units
	1960	11,151 units
	1961	5,449 units
total	24,676 units	

Production of the 180Dc [120 III] (from June 1961 until October
1962)

was in	1961	4,822 units
	1962	7,000 units
total	11,822 units	

Model 180D (1953-1962)

The 180D was introduced after the 180 gasoline-engined sedan. Early production of this diesel-engined model was in October 1953 and regular production began in February 1954.

Again, in all respects, body and chassis of these two models were identical. The new unit frame construction and redesigned front end of this recently introduced four-door sedan was shared by both types. The 180D diesel engine was identical to that of the 170Db, but the rear axle ratio had been reduced and in September 1955 the engine output was raised to 43 horsepower. In April 1958 wind wings were placed on the front door windows, but otherwise the body remained the same as previously used.

The 180Db model production began in July 1959 and was to continue until August 1961. Larger diameter brakes, a wider radiator shell, and no vertical bumper bars were the only alterations.

The 18Dc, built from June 1961 until October 1962 had the larger engine. Displacing 1,988 cubic centimeters, it developed 48 horsepower at 3,800 revolutions per minute. Compression ratio was raised to 21 to 1.

Specifications

	180D / 180Db	180Dc
Engine type	4 cyl diesel (OM 636)	4 cyl diesel (OM 621)
Bore and stroke	75 x 100mm (2.96 x 3.94 in)	87 x 83.6mm (3.43 x 3.29 in)
Displacement	1767 cc (107.7 cu in)	1988 cc (121 cu in)
Power output	40 hp (DIN) @ 3200 rpm 46 hp (SAE) @ 3500 rpm from Sept. '55: 43 hp @ 3500	48 hp (DIN) @ 3800 rpm
Compression ratio	19:1	21:1
Torque	10.3mgk @2000 rpm (75ft/lb)	11mkg @2200rpm (80ft/lb)
Fuel injection	Bosch injection pump (pre-combustion chamber)	
Engine speed at 100 km/hr	3330 rpm	3330 rpm
Gear ratios	I. 4.05:1 (15.0) II. 2.38:1 (8.81) III. 1.53:1 (5.66) IV. 1.00:1 (3.70)	I. 4.05:1 (15.0) II. 2.38:1 (8.81) III. 1.53:1 (5.66) IV. 1.00:1 (3.70)
Rear axle ratio	3.70 (37:10)	3.70 (37:10)
Chassis	unit frame and body	unit frame and body
Suspension	independent front, swing axle rear, with coil springs from Sept. '55: single swing axle	rear: single swing axle
Brakes and area	drum, 816 cm² (126.5 sq in)	drum, 1064 cm² (164.9 sq in)
Wheelbase	2650mm (104.3 in)	2650mm (104.3 in)
Track, front/rear	1430/1475mm (56.3/58.1 in)	1430/1475mm (56.3/58.1 in)
Length	4485mm (176.6 in)	4485mm (176.6 in)
Width	1740mm (68.5 in)	1740mm (68.5 in)
Height	1560mm (61.4 in)	1560mm (61.4 in)
Ground clearance	185mm (7.3 in)	185mm (7.3 in)
Tires	6.40 x 13	6.40 x 13
Turning circle	11.5 meters (38 ft)	11.5 meters (38 ft)
Steering type and ratio	recirculating ball, 18.5:1	recirculating ball, 18.5:1
Weight	1220 kg (2684 lbs)	1220 kg (2684 lbs)
Maximum speed	112 km/hr (70 mph) from Sept. '55: 115 km/hr	120 km/hr (75 mph)
Acceleration	39 sec 0-100 km from Sept. '55: 37 sec	36 sec 0-100 km
Fuel consumption	8 liters/100 km (29.3 mpg)	8 liters/100 km (29.3 mpg)
Fuel tank capacity	56 liters (14.8 gallons)	56 liters (14.8 gallons)

Model 300SL (1954-1963)

The 300SL sports car went into regular production in August 1954, but a more austere version had appeared on the international sports car racing scene in 1952. After an interval of many years, the company had decided to enter competition again and the 300SL was built. The designation SL (sport-light) described a new design in which the frame was replaced by a light but very stiff structure of a lattice pattern, made of thin welded steel tubing, and the outer cover was also very light since the lattice structure bears all stress.

The engine, developed from the 300S model, was mounted slanting 45 degrees for a lower hood line in order to allow the driver and passenger a better view ahead.

First tested in international competition in sports car races in Switzerland, at Le Mans, the Nürburgring, and the Panamericana in Mexico, the car earned its laurels. The magnificent victories, and the entire history of the 300SL, are related in another book by this author.

The production car incorporated many improvements gained from the racing experience. One of the striking features was the direct fuel injection which gave the 2,996 cubic centimeter six-cylinder engine 215 horsepower (240 SAE) at 5,800 revolutions per minute, and a maximum speed of 235 kilometers with the 3.64 rear axle and 260 kilometers (162 miles) per hour with the 3.25 axle fitted. The turbo brake drums were self-cooling and servo-assisted and were the same as on the 300S model. The speeds in the gears were 75 kilometers (47 miles) in first, 128 km (80 m) in second, 186 km (116 m) in third, and 240 kilometers (149 miles) in fourth at 6,000 revolutions per minute.

The 300SL roadster with conventional type doors was first shown at the Geneva Show in March 1957 and put into regular production in May. It was basically the same car as the gull-wing coupe, but the lower door line was closer to the ground and getting in and out was greatly facilitated. In many ways a superior sports car than the former, it never achieved the enthusiastic support of the

original version, although actually more cars were produced during the seven years it was built.

The tubular frame was somewhat heavier because of the absence of the coupe body; the car weighed 1,330 kilograms to the 1,295 of the former, an increase of 77 pounds. The engine later had the competition camshaft installed with a higher compression ratio, 9.5 to 1, and was rated at 250 SAE horsepower at 6,200 revolutions per minute. The German specifications listed 215 horsepower at 5,800 revolutions per minute and the 8.55 compression ratio, as the earlier coupe model had. The U.S. cars also had the 3.89 rear axle ratio.

The various axle ratios gave the following maximum speeds: 3.25 at 155 miles per hour; 3.42 at 150, 3.64 at 146, 3.89 at 137, and 4.11 ratio at 129 miles per hour.

A hard top for the convertible roadster became available in September 1958 at extra cost, and in March 1961, four-wheel disc brakes were installed as a regular production item.

Prices and Production

The 300SL coupe sold for . . . . .DM 29,000
Price in the United States was first . . . .$ 6,820
   then rose to (finally) . . . .$ 8,902
The 300SL roadster sold for . . . . . . .DM 32,500
   removable hardtop. . . . . .DM   1,500
Price in the United States was first . . . .$ 10,970
   then . . . .$ 11,099
   and. . . . .$ 11,573

Production of the 300 SL coupe [198 I] (from
August 1954 until May 1957)

	was in	1954	146 units
		1955	867 units
		1956	311 units
		1957	76 units
	total		1,400 units

Production of the 300SL roadster [198 II] (from
February/May 1957 until February 1963)

	was in	1957	554 units
		1958	324 units
		1959	211 units
		1960	249 units
		1961	250 units
		1962	244 units
		1963	26 units
	total		1,858 units

Specifications

	300SL (coupe)	300SL (roadster)
Engine type	6 cyl overhead camshaft (45° slanted to the left) (M 198)	
Bore and stroke	85 x 88mm (3.35 x 3.46 in)	85 x 88mm (3.35 x 3.46 in)
Displacement	2996 cc (182.7 cu in)	2996 cc (182.7 cu in)
Power output	215 hp (DIN) @ 5800 rpm (240 hp SAE) (for U.S.: 250 hp @ 6200 rpm)	
Compression ratio	8.55:1	9.5:1
Torque	28 mkg @ 4600 rpm (217 ft/lb @ 4800 rpm)	228 ft/lb
Fuel injection	Bosch injection pump	Bosch injection pump
Engine speed at 100 km/hr	3000 rpm	3000 rpm
Gear ratios	I. 3.34:1 (12.15) II. 1.97:1 (7.18) III. 1.385:1 (5.03) IV. 1.00:1 (3.64)	I. 3.34:1 (12.15) for U.S. II. 1.97:1 (7.18) (13.0) III. 1.385:1 (5.03) (7.66) IV. 1.00:1 (3.64) (5.40) (3.89)
Rear axle ratio	3.64; also 3.25; 3.42; 3.89; 4.11 upon request	
Chassis	tubular space frame with light alloy body	
Suspension	independent front, swing axle rear, with coil springs	
Brakes and area	drum, 1470 cm² (227.9 sq in) servo assisted; from Mar. '61 discs	
Wheelbase	2400mm (94.5 in)	2400mm (94.5 in)
Track, front/rear	1385/1435mm (54.5/56.5 in)	1398/1448mm (55.0/57.0 in)
Length	4520mm (178 in)	4570mm (180 in)
Width	1790mm (70.5 in)	1790mm (70.5 in)
Height	1300mm (51.2 in)	1300mm (51.2 in)
Ground clearance	130mm (5.1 in)	130mm (5.1 in)
Tires	6.50 x 15 super sport	6.70 x 15 super sport
Turning circle	11.4 meters (37 ft)	11.4 meters (37 ft)
Steering type and ratio	recirculating ball, 17.3:1 (3 turns)	recirculating ball, 17.3:1 (3 turns)
Weight	1295 kg (2849 lbs)	1330 kg (2926 lbs)
Maximum speed	3.64 axle: 235 km/hr (145 mph); 3.42-250 km/hr (155 mph); 3.25-260 km/hr (165 mph)	
Acceleration	8.7 sec 0-100 km/hr	8.1 sec 0-100 km/hr (for U.S. 7.2 sec)
Fuel consumption	17 liters, super / 100 km (13.7 mpg)	
Fuel tank capacity	130 liters (34 U.S. gallons)	100 liters (26 U.S. gallons)

Prices and Production

The 190SL roadster, with cloth top, sold for . . . . .DM 16,500
    with removable hard top. . . . . .DM 17,100
    with both types top . . . . .DM 17,650
In the U.S. the 190SL roadster sold in 1958
    East coast . . . .$ 5,020
    West coast . . . .$ 5,129

Production of the 190SL [121 II] (from January/May 1955 until
February 1963)

was in	1955	1,727 units
	1956	4,032 units
	1957	3,332 units
	1958	2,722 units
	1959	3,949 units
	1960	3,977 units
	1961	3,792 units
	1962	2,246 units
	1963	104 units
	total	25,881 units

Model 190SL (1955-1963)

The 190SL model was announced early in 1954 as a smaller version of the 300SL, but initial production did not start until January 1955, when several important modifications had been made on the original design. This touring-sports car was based on the 180 model sedan and used the basic, but slightly altered, self-supporting frame-floor unit construction with the subframe assembly carrying the engine. The open roadster model needed greater support than the four-door sedan model.

The sporty body of the 190SL resembled that of the larger SL model but had regular fitted doors. A steering column gear shift lever operated the four-speed synchro-meshed gear box. Speeds in gears were 46, 81, 128, and 190 kilometers (28, 50, 80, and 118 miles) per hour. Real leather bucket-type seats added greatly to the comfort and appearance of the silvery sports car.

The four-cylinder engine had a displacement of 1,897 cubic centimeters and a compression ratio of 8.5 to 1. The overhead camshaft engine, equipped with two Solex horizontal carburetors, developed 105 horsepower at 5,700 revolutions per minute (in the U.S. version 125 at 6,000). Maximum speed was given as 171 kilometers (106 miles) per hour. Torque was 101 ft/lbs.

The 190SL was advertised to sell in New York for $3,998 in 1955. The copy indicated a 125-horsepower engine and top speed of 118 miles per hour for this "blood brother" of the fabulous 300SL.

In September 1959 a new style hard top was designed with larger window area giving improved vision.

Specifications

	190SL
Engine type	4 cyl (M 121)
Bore and stroke	85 x 83.6mm (3.35 x 3.29 in)
Displacement	1897 cc (115.7 cu in)
Power output	105 hp (DIN) @ 5700 rpm (120 hp (SAE) @ 5700 rpm)
Compression ratio	8.5:1 from Sept. '59: 8.8:1
Torque	14.5 mkg @ 3200 rpm (105 ft/lb @ 3200 rpm)
Carburetion	2 dual downdraft carburetors Solex 44 PHH
Engine speed at 100 km/hr	3350 rpm
Gear ratios	I. 3.52:1 (13.7) II. 2.32:1 (9.02) III. 1.52:1 (5.92) IV. 1.00:1 (3.89)
Rear axle ratio	3.90 (39:10)
Chassis	unit frame and body
Suspension	independent front, single joint swing axle rear, with coil springs
Brakes and area	drum, 1064 cm^2 (164.9 sq in) servo optional
Wheelbase	2400mm (94.5 in)
Track, front/rear	1430/1475mm (56.2/58.1 in)
Length	4220mm (166.1 in)
Width	1740mm (68.5 in)
Height	1320mm (52 in)
Ground clearance	185mm (7.3 in)
Tires	6.40 x 13 sport
Turning circle	11 meters (36.1 ft)
Steering type and ratio	recirculating ball, 18.5:1
Weight	roadster: 1160 kg (2552 lbs) coupe: 1180 kg (2596 lbs)
Maximum speed	171 km/hr (106 mph)
Acceleration	14.5 sec 0-100 km
Fuel consumption	12.5 liters super/100 km (18.75 mpg)
Fuel tank capacity	65 liter (17 gallons)

Pre-production model, January 1955

33

Prices and Production

The 190 four-door sedan in 1956-1961 sold for. . . . . . .DM   9,450
    Servo brakes available at additional. . . . . .DM   300
The 190c four-door sedan sold in 1961 for. . . . . .DM   9,950
    from April 1962 . . . . .DM 10,600
    Servo brakes available at additional. . . . . .DM   300
    (until August 1963)
    Power steering (from May 1964) . . . . .DM   550
    Automatic transmission (from August 1962) . . . . . .DM   1,400

Production of the 190 model [121 I] (from March 1956 until August 1959)

was in	1956	16,001 units
	1957	22,578 units
	1958	15,791 units
	1959	6,975 units
	total	61,345 units

Production of the 190b model [121 III] (from June 1959 until August 1961)

was in	1959	6,613 units
	1960	12,986 units
	1961	8,864 units
	total	28,463 units

Production of the 190c model [110] (from April 1961 until August 1965)

was in	1961	9,249 units
	1962	31,275 units
	1963	35,457 units
	1964	33,776 units
	1965	20,797 units
	total	130,554 units

Model 190 (1956-1965)

The 190 sedan, introduced at the Frankfurt Auto Show in 1956, was one of three new models shown to the public at that time. The body style was the same as that of the 180 sedan, but the new single overhead camshaft four-cylinder engine of 1,897 cubic centimeters (actually a de-tuned version of the 190SL power unit) developed 75 horsepower at 4,600 revolutions per minute. It was mounted on four points on the U-frame, resulting in greater quietness of operation. Interior furnishings of the 190 sedan were somewhat superior to those of the 180 model but outwardly the only distinguishing feature was a decorative chrome line around the body.

The 190b model, built from June 1959 on, had a wider radiator shell and the bumper had no vertical bumper guard bar.

The 190c model, produced from April 1961 until August 1965, was quite different from the preceding models of the same designation. It was longer, larger, and lower, and had the body style of the 220 models of that period, with the slight tail fins. But it had a slightly shorter hood line, round lights, and simple bumpers.

From August 1963 on, the model was equipped with disc brakes and a twin circuit hydraulic system. An automatic transmission was also available from August 1962 on at extra cost.

Specifications

	190	190b	190c
Engine type	4 cyl overhead camshaft (M 121)	4 cyl overhead camshaft (M 121)	4 cyl overhead camshaft (M 121)
Bore and stroke	85 x 83.6mm (3.35 x 3.29 in)	85 x 83.6mm (3.35 x 3.29 in)	85 x 83.6mm (3.34 x 3.29 in)
Displacement	1897 cc (115.7 cu in)	1897 cc (115.7 cu in)	1897 cc (115.7 cu in)
Power output	75 hp (DIN) @ 4600 rpm (84 SAE hp)	80 hp (DIN) @ 4800 rpm	80 hp (DIN) @ 500 rpm (90 hp SAE @ 5200 rpm)
Compression ratio	7.5:1	8.5:1	8.7:1
Torque	13.9 mkg @ 2800 rpm (101 ft/lb)	14.2 mkg @ 2800 rpm (103 ft/lb)	14.5 mkg @ 2500 rpm (15.6 mkg @ 2700 rpm SAE 112.9 ft/lb)
Carburation	1 downdraft carburetor Solex 32 PAITA	1 downdraft carburetor Solex 32 PAITA	1 downdraft carburetor Solex 34 PJCB
Engine speed at 100 km/hr	3300 rpm	3300 rpm	3300 rpm
Gear ratios	I. 4.05:1 II. 2.38:1 III. 1.53:1 IV. 1.00:1	I. 4.05:1 II. 2.38:1 III. 1.53:1 IV. 1.00:1	I. 4.05:1 automatic 3.98:1 II. 2.28:1 2.52:1 III. 1.53:1 1.58:1 IV. 1.00:1 1.00:1
Rear axle ratio	4.10	4.10	4.08
Chassis	unit frame and body	unit frame and body	unit frame and body
Suspension	independent front, single joint swing axle rear, with coil springs (from 1963; air suspension, optional)		
Brakes and area	drum, 1064 cm² (164.9 sq in) servo optional		drum, 1064 cm² (164.9 sq in) servo assisted from Aug. '63; disc, front
Wheelbase	2650mm (104.3 in)	2650mm (104.3 in)	2700mm (106.3 in)
Track, front/rear	1430/1475mm (56.2/58.1 in)	1430/1475mm (56.2/58.1 in)	1468/1485mm (58/58.5in) from Aug.'63 1482/1465mm
Length	4485mm (176.6 in)	4500mm (177.2 in)	4730mm (186.5 in)
Width	1740mm (68.5 in)	1740mm (68.5 in)	1795mm (70.7 in)
Height	1560mm (61.4 in)	1560mm (61.4 in)	1495,mm (58.8 in)
Ground clearance	185mm (7.3 in)	185,mm (7.3 in)	185mm (7.3 in)
Tires	6.40 x 13	6.40 x 13	7.00 x 13
Turning circle	11.5 meters (38 ft)	11.5 meters (38 ft)	11.8-11.6 meters (38 ft)
Steering type and ratio	recirculating ball, 18.5:1 (3.75 turns)	recirculating ball, 18.5:1 (3.75 turns)	recirculating ball, 21.4:1 (3.75 turns) from May '64: servo assist 17.3:1 (3.2 turns)
Weight	1240 kg (2728 lbs)	1240 kg (2728 lbs)	1280 kg (2816 lbs)
Maximum speed	139 km/hr (86 mph)	144 km/hr (89 mph)	150 km/hr (93 mph) automatic: 145 km/hr (90 mph)
Acceleration	20.5 sec 0-100 km	19 sec 0-100 km	18 sec 0-100 km/hr automatic: 22 sec 0-100 km/hr
Fuel consumption	11.5 liters, super/100 km (20.4 mpg)		11.5 liters, super/100 km (20.4 mpg) automatic: 12.5 liters (18.75 mpg)
Fuel tank capacity	56 liters (14.8 gallons)	56 liters (14.8 gallons)	52 liters (13.5 gallons)

Model 219 (1956-1959)

The 219 sedan was the second model introduced at the Frankfurt Auto Show in 1956. The body style was identical to that of the 190 sedan, but the wheelbase was slightly larger, 2,750 millimeters to 2,650 millimeters for the 190 (3.937 inches longer). The six-cylinder engine was the same as that of the former 220 sedan, the proven 2,195 cubic centimeter unit developing 85 horsepower (92 SAE) at 4,800 revolutions per minute. Power output was increased in August 1957 to 90 horsepower (100 SAE), and the compression ratio from 7.6 to 8.7 to 1. With the increase in power, a slight increase in fuel consumption was also experienced, naturally, but only by one liter for 100 kilometers.

The 219 model was considered the middle range of the three newly developed sedans and the lowest priced six-cylinder one. The maximum speed, and cruising speed, was given as 148 kilometers (92 miles) per hour, with the 190 model doing 139 kilometers (86 miles) per hour and the 220S having a maximum speed of 99.4 miles, or 160 kilometers per hour.

As an optional extra, a hydraulic transmission was available. In this Hydrak system made by Fichtel and Sachs, a hydraulic coupling was used in connection with a conventional clutch automatically controlled. When the driver moved the gear lever, the clutch action was initiated. The system made for easier driving and provided engine braking at all times. It ensured smoothness of operation and saved the engine.

Prices and Production

The 219 four-door sedan sold for . . . . .DM 10,500
    Servo brakes available at an additional . . . . .DM   300
    Hydrak transmission . . . . .DM   450
Price in the U.S. was in 1956 . . . .$ 3,889

Production of the 219 model [105] (from March 1956 until July 1959)

was in 1956	5,474 units
1957	8,505 units
1958	9,296 units
1959	4,570 units
total	27,845 units

Specifications

	219
Engine type	6 cyl overhead camshaft (M 180)
Bore and stroke	80 x 72.8mm (3.15 x 2.87 in)
Displacement	2195 cc (133.9 cu in)
Power output	85 hp (DIN) @ 4800 rpm (92 hp SAE) from Aug. '57: 90 hp (DIN) (100 hp SAE)
Compression ratio	7.6:1 from Aug. '57: 8.7:1
Torque	16 mkg @ 2400 rpm (116 ft/lb) from Aug. '57: 17 mkg (123 ft/lb)
Carburetion	1 dual downdraft carburetor Solex 32 PAATJ
Engine speed at 100 km/hr	3320 rpm
Gear ratios	I. 3.52:1 (14.4) II. 2.32:1 (9.51) III. 1.52:1 (6.23) IV. 1.00:1 (4.10)
Rear axle ratio	4.10 from Aug. '57: 3.90
Chassis	unit frame and body
Suspension	independent front, single joint swing axle rear, with coil springs
Brakes and area	drum, 1064 cm^2 (164.9 sq in)
Wheelbase	2750mm (108.3 in)
Track, front/rear	1430/1470mm (56.2/57.9 in)
Length	4680mm (184.3 in)
Width	1740mm (68.5 in)
Height	1560mm (61.4 in)
Ground clearance	185mm (7.3 in)
Tires	6.40 x 13
Turning circle	11.5 meters (38 ft)
Steering type and ratio	recirculating ball, 21.4:1 (4 turns)
Weight	1290 kg (2838 lbs)
Maximum speed	148 km/hr (92 mph)
Acceleration	17 sec 0-100 km
Fuel consumption	14.5 liters/100 km (16.2 mpg) from Aug. '57 13.5 liters
Fuel tank capacity	56 liters (14.8 gallons)

Prices and Production

The 220S four-door sedan sold for . . . . .DM 12,500
The 220S two-door convertible coupe sold for . . . . . . .DM 21,500
The 220S two-door hard top coupe sold for . . . . .DM 21,500
   Hydrak transmission . . . . .DM   450
Price in the United States was in 1956. . . . .$ 4,283

Production of the 220S [180 II] (from March 1956 until August 1959)

was in	1956	10,525 units
	1957	15,459 units
	1958	20,181 units
	1959	9,114 units
	total	55,279 units

Production of the 220S convertible and coupe [180 II] (from July 1956 until October 1959)

was in	1956	297 units
	1957	1,066 units
	1958	1,280 units
	1959	786 units
	total	3,429 units

Model 220S (1956-1959)

The sedan was the third of the new models shown to the public at the Frankfurt Show in 1956. It was also the most powerful one of the trio and the most expensive one as well. The 2,195 cubic centimeter six-cylinder engine was of the same size as that of the 219, but it developed 100 horsepower (112 SAE) at 4,800 revolutions per minute. From August 1957 on, with the compression ratio increased from 7.6 to 8.7 to 1, it developed 106 horsepower at 5,200 revolutions per minute. In the United States the engine was rated at 120 SAE horsepower. The Hydrak automatic transmission was also available from August 1957 on at an additional cost of DM 450.

The 220S was considered the refined successor of the 220a model, but the body style had not undergone many changes. A convertible appeared in May 1956 and the hard top coupe in 1957.

Specifications

	220S
Engine type	6 cyl overhead camshaft (M 180)
Bore and stroke	80 x 72.8mm (3.15 x 2.87 in)
Displacement	2195 cc (133.9 cu in)
Power output	100 hp (DIN) @ 4800 rpm (112 hp SAE) from Aug. '57: 106 @ 5200 (124 hp SAE)
Compression ratio	7.6:1 from Aug. '57: 8.7:1
Torque	16.5 mkg @ 3500 rpm (119 ft/lb) from Aug. '57: 17.5 mkg (127 ft/lb)
Carburetion	2 downdraft carburetors Solex 32 PAJTA
Engine speed at 100 km/hr	3320 rpm
Gear ratio	I. 3.52:1 II. 2.32:1 III. 1.52:1 IV. 1.00:1
Rear axle ratio	4.10
Chassis	unit frame and body
Suspension	independent front, single joint swing axle rear, with coil springs
Brakes and area	drum, 1064 cm^2 (164.9 sq in) servo assisted
Wheelbase	2820mm (111 in); coupe and convertible: 2,700mm (106.3 in)
Track, front/rear	1430/1470mm (56.2/57.9 in)
Length	4750mm (187 in); coupe and convertible: 4670mm (183.9 in)
Width	1740mm (68.5 in); coupe and convertible: 1765mm (69.5 in)
Height	1560mm (61.4 in); coupe and convertible: 1530mm (60.2 in)
Ground clearance	185mm (7.3 in)
Tires	6.70 x 13 sport
Turning circle	11.7 meters (38 ft); coupe and convertible: 11.4 meters (37 ft)
Steering type and ratio	recirculating ball, 21.4:1 (4 turns)
Weight	1350 kg (2970 lbs); coupe: 1410 kg (3102 lbs); convertible: 1450 kg (3219 lbs)
Maximum speed	160 km/hr (99.5 mph)
Acceleration	17 sec 0-100 km
Fuel consumption	13.5 liters super/100 km (17.4 mpg) coupe and convertible: 14 liters super
Fuel tank capacity	64 liters (16.9 gallons)

Prices and Production

The 220SE four-door sedan sold for . . . . .DM 14,400
The 220SE two-door convertible sold for. . . . . .DM 23,400
The 220SE two-door coupe sold for . . . . .DM 23,400
    Hydrak transmission . . . . .DM   450
The 220SE convertible or coupe sold
    after August 1959 for. .DM 23,200

Production of the 220SE [128] (from April/October 1958 until August 1959)

was in	1958	201 units
	1959	1,773 units
	total	1,974 units

Production of the 220SE convertible and coupe [128] (from July/October 1958 until November 1960)

was in	1958	114 units
	1959	628 units
	1960	1,200 units
	total	1,942 units

Model 220SE (1958-1960)

The 220SE was first introduced in September 1958. Early pre-production was actually begun in April of that year, but the regular production lines did not get underway until October. The sedan had the same body style and furnishing of the 220S and was only different in the fuel-injected engine. The regular carburetor engine was equipped with two Solex downdraft carburetors and developed 100 horsepower (112 SAE) for the 220S; while the injection engine, using a Bosch two-plunger injection pump, developed 120 horsepower (134 SAE). It was also considerably more flexible than the carburetor unit.

The manifold injection system cost about $400 more to produce than the regular carburetion system, but the engineers estimated that it resulted in 18 percent more power, 5 percent greater torque, and reduced fuel consumption by 8 percent.

The air collection chamber and six intake pipes fed the air to the individual ports and fuel was injected just ahead of the junction of the manifold and the cylinder head. A calibrated jet was used for each individual cylinder and the fuel was being fed from the two plunger pumps which operated at engine speed. Injection was also controlled by temperature and barometric pressure. It was not a direct injection, but a manifold injection system.

The 220SE two-door convertible and coupe models were also shown at the same time as the sedan model. When in August 1959 production of the sedan ceased, the convertible and coupe models remained in production until the end of 1960, but were equipped with the newer, 120-horsepower fuel injection engine of the 220SEb type.

Specifications

	220SE
Engine type	6 cyl overhead camshaft (M 180)
Bore and stroke	80 x 72.8mm (3.15 x 2.87 in)
Displacement	2195 cc (133.9 cu in)
Power output	115 hp (DIN) @ 4800 rpm (134 hp SAE @ 5000 rpm)
Compression ratio	8.7:1
Torque	19 mkg @ 3800 rpm (152 ft/lb @ 4100)
Fuel injection	Bosch two-plunger pump (into manifold)
Engine speed at 100 km/hr	3320 rpm
Gear ratios	I. 3.52:1 U.S. cars: I. 3.65:1 (14.9) II. 2.32:1 II. 2.36:1 (9.68) III. 1.52:1 III. 1.53:1 (6.27) IV. 1.00:1 IV. 1.00:1 (4.10)
Rear axle ratio	4.10
Chassis	unit frame and body
Suspension	independent front, single joint swing axle rear, with coil springs
Brakes and area	drum, 1064 cm² (164.9 sq in) servo assisted
Wheelbase	2820mm (111 in); coupe and convertible: 2700mm (106.3 in)
Track, front/rear	1430/1470mm (56.2/57.9 in)
Length	4750mm (187 in); coupe and convertible: 4670mm (183.9 in)
Width	1740mm (68.5 in); coupe and convertible: 1765mm (69.5 in)
Height	1560mm (61.4 in); coupe and convertible: 1530mm (60.2 in)
Ground clearance	185mm (7.3 in)
Tires	6.70 x 13 sport
Turning circle	11.7 meters (38 ft); coupe and convertible: 11.4 meters (37 ft)
Steering type and ratio	recirculating ball, 21.4:1 (4 turns)
Weight	1370 kg (3014 lbs); coupe: 1430 kg (3146 lbs); convertible: 1470 kg (3234 lbs)
Maximum speed	160 km/hr (99.5 mph)
Acceleration	15 sec 0-100 km
Fuel consumption	13 liters super/100 km (18 mpg); coupe and convertible: 13.5 liters (17.4 mpg)
Fuel tank capacity	62 liters (16.4 gallons)

Prices and Production

The 190D four-door sedan sold in 1958-1961 for . . . . .DM   9,950
The 190Dc four-door sedan in 1961 sold for. . . . . . . .DM 10,450
   from April 1962 for. . . . . .DM 11,100
   Power steering (from May 1964) . . . . .DM   550
   Automatic transmission (from September 1963) . . . .DM   1,400

Production of the 190D model [121 I] (from August 1958 until July 1959)

	was in	1958	5,469 units
		1959	15,160 units
		total	20,629 units

Production of the 190Db [121 II] (from June 1959 until September 1961)

	was in	1959	13,709 units
		1960	29,116 units
		1961	18,484 units
		total	61,309 units

Production of the 190Dc model [110] (from April/June 1961 until August 1965)

	was in	1961	12,882 units
		1962	45,414 units
		1963	60,784 units
		1964	64,422 units
		1965	42,143 units
		total	225,645 units

Model 190D (1958-1965)

The 190D model followed the gasoline-powered 190 model more than two years later. It was not put into production until August 1958. That year, the 180D was still being sold; in fact, over 26,000 units were produced and nearly 10,000 of them were sold the next year. Along with the new 190D model, the 180Db appeared in 1959 and the 180Dc in 1961. This smaller version (and older body style) was still a very popular car and in great demand. The 180D and 180Db had the 1,767 cubic centimeter displacement engine, while the 190D and 190Db had the larger 1,897 cubic centimeter diesel unit. The 180Dc had a 1,988 cubic centimeter engine and the 190Dc, as well as the 200D later, shared that same power plant.

The 190D model had the 1,897 cubic centimeter engine of 50 horsepower at 4,000 revolutions per minute. It was completely redesigned from the previous one, had a shorter stroke and single overhead camshaft instead of the older pushrod, long-stroke engine which was still being used in the 180D model. The maximum speed of the 190D was 126 kilometers (78 miles) per hour.

To dramatically introduce the new, larger, and more powerful diesel engine to the public, a car was entered to compete in the tortuous 8,727-mile African Rallye from Algiers to Capetown. Karl Kling drove the car to victory, averaging 55.5 miles per hour across the Dark Continent.

The 190Db, built from August 1959 to August 1961, shared the body with its gasoline engined counterpart, with the wider radiator grille and simpler bumper without guards.

The 190Dc, built until August 1965, was similar to the 190c. It had the same dimensions and shared that same newer body style with the tail fins, longer, larger, and lower than the previous one.

Specifications

	190D / 190Db	190Dc
Engine type	4 cyl diesel, single overhead camshaft (OM 621)	
Bore and stroke	85 x 83.6mm (3.35 x 3.29 in)	87 x 83.6mm (3.43 x 3.29 in)
Displacement	1897 cc (115.7 cu in)	1988 cc (121.27 cu in)
Power output	50 hp (DIN) @ 4000 rpm (55 hp SAE)	55 hp (DIN) @ 4200 rpm (60 hp SAE)
Compression ratio	21:1	21:1
Torque	11mkg @2200 rpm(79.5 ft/lbs)	11.5 mkg 2400 rpm 12 mkg SAE 87 ft/lbs)
Fuel injection	Bosch injection pump pre-combustion chamber	Bosch injection pump
Engine speed at 100 km/hr	3300 rpm	3300 rpm
Gear ratios	I. 4.05:1 II. 2.38:1 III. 1.53:1 IV. 1.00:1	I. 4.05:1 automatic I. 3.98:1 II. 2.28:1 II. 2.52:1 III. 1.53:1 III. 1.58:1 IV. 1.00:1 IV. 1.00:1
Rear axle ratio	3.70	3.92
Chassis	unit frame and body	unit frame and body
Suspension	independent front, single joint swing axle rear, with coil springs from 1963: air suspension, optional	
Brakes and area	drum, 1064 cm² (164.9 sq in)	drum, 1064 cm² (164.9 sq in) servo assisted from Aug. '63: disc, front
Wheelbase	2650mm (104.3 in)	2700mm (106.3 in)
Track, front/rear	1430/1475mm (56.2/58.1 in)	1468/1485mm (58/58.5 in) from Aug.'63: 1482/1485mm (58.3/58.5 in)
Length	4485mm (176.6 in) b: 4500mm (177.2 in)	4730mm (186.5 in)
Width	1740mm (68.5 in)	1795mm (70.7 in)
Height	1560mm (61.4 in)	1495mm (58.8 in)
Ground clearance	185mm (7.3 in)	185mm (7.3 in)
Tires	6.40 x 13	7.00 x 13
Turning circle	11.5 meters (38 ft)	11.8-11.6 meters (38 ft)
Steering type and ratio	recirculating ball, 18.5:1 (3.75 turns)	recirculating ball, 21.4:1; from May '64: servo assisted 17.3:1 (3.2 turns)
Weight	1250 kg (2750 lbs)	1320 kg (2904 lbs)
Maximum speed	126 km/hr (78 mph)	130 km/hr (81 mph); automatic 127 km/hr (79 mph)
Acceleration	29 sec 0-100 km	29 sec 0-100 km/hr; automatic 30 sec 0-100 km/hr
Fuel consumption	8.5 liters/100 km (27.75 mpg)	9 liters/100 km (26 mpg); automatic 10 liters/100 km (23.5 mpg)
Fuel tank capacity	56 liters (14.8 gallons)	52 liters (13.5 gallons)

Prices and Production

The 220b four-door sedan sold for . . . . .DM 11,500
    from April 1962 for. . . . . .DM 12,160
    Power steering . . . . .DM   550
    Hydrak transmission (until 1961). . . . .' . . .DM   450
    Automatic transmission (from August 1962) . . . . . .DM 1,400
Price in the United States was . . . .$ 4,370

Production of the 220b [111/1] (from May/August 1959 until
August 1965)

was in	1959	3,375 units
	1960	13,127 units
	1961	14,842 units
	1962	11,618 units
	1963	10,492 units
	1964	11,327 units
	1965	4,910 units
	total	69,691 units

Model 220 (1959-1965)

The 220b model sedan, shown to the public at the Frankfurt Auto Show in 1959, was one of four models which shared the new body style. The four-door sedans had a wider radiator shell, a longer body (4.875 millimeters, 191.9 inches, overall length) with slight rear fins, wrap-around windshield, and wide rear window, as well as dual vertically positioned headlights. Bumpers had a narrower one above the standard sized one.

The 220b model was the successor to the 219 sedan, which was then discontinued. The 2,195 cubic centimeter six-cylinder engine developed 95 horsepower (105 SAE) and had the higher compression ratio (8.7 to 1) of the later 219 production models. Maximum speed was also increased from 148 to 160 kilometers (99.4 miles) per hour.

The Hydrak transmission was available until 1961 and after August 1962 an automatic transmission became an optional extra item. A year later, in August 1963, the car was fitted with disc brakes on the front wheels and a hydraulic dual braking system. Power brakes were also available.

Specifications

	220			
Engine type	6 cyl overhead camshaft (M 180)			
Bore and stroke	80 x 72.8mm (3.16 x 2.87 in)			
Displacement	2195 cc (133.9 cu in)			
Power output	95 hp (DIN) @ 4800 rpm (105 hp SAE @ 5000 rpm)			
Compression ratio	8.7:1			
Torque	17.2 mkg @ 3200 rpm (18.4 mkg 133.2 ft/lb @ 3300)			
Carburetion	2 downdraft carburetors Solex 34 PJCB			
Engine speed at 100 km/hr	3300 rpm			
Gear ratios	I. 3.64:1	automatic	I.	3.98:1
	II. 2.36:1 (later 2.28:1)		II.	2.52:1
	III. 1.53:1		III.	1.58:1
	IV. 1.00:1		IV.	1.00:1
Rear axle ratio	3.90		4.10	
Chassis	unit frame and body			
Suspension	independent front, single joint swing axle rear, with coil springs			
Brakes and area	drum, 1064 cm² (164.9 sq in), servo assisted, optional from Aug. '63 disc, front			
Wheelbase	2750mm (108.3 in)			
Track, front/rear	1470/1485mm (57.9/58.5 in) from Aug. '63: 1482/1485mm (58.3/58.5 in)			
Length	4875mm (191.9 in)			
Width	1795mm (70.7 in)			
Height	1500mm (59.1 in)			
Ground clearance	165mm (6.5 in)			
Tires	6.70 x 13; from 1960: 7.25 x 13			
Turning circle	12.1-11.9 meters (39 ft)			
Steering type and ratio	recirculating ball, 21.4:1 (3.75 turns)			
Weight	1320 kg (2904 lbs)			
Maximum speed	160 km/hr (99.5 mph)			
Acceleration	16 sec 0-100 km/hr			
Fuel consumption	14 liters, super/100 km (16.75 mpg); automatic: 15 liters, super (15.6 mpg)			
Fuel tank capacity	65 liters (17.2 gallons)			

Model 220S (1959-1965)

The 220S, first shown publicly in late 1959, was the second model which also shared the new body style of the sedans. All outside dimensions were the same as that of the other three models.

The six-cylinder engine developed 110 horsepower (124 SAE) and maximum speed was given as 165 kilometers (102.5 miles) per hour. Disc brakes on the front wheels were fitted from April 1962, and from August 1963 a hydraulic dual braking system was installed.

Prices and Production

The 220Sb four-door sedan sold for . . . . .DM 13,250
    from April 1962 for. . . . . .DM 13,750
    Power steering . . . . .DM   550
    Hydrak transmission (until 1961). . . . . .DM   450
    Automatic transmission (from August 1962) . . . . . .DM 1,400
Price in the United States was . . . .$ 5,120

Production of the 220Sb [111/2] (from May/August 1959 until July 1965)

	was in	1959	7,267 units
		1960	26,642 units
		1961	32,238 units
		1962	26,077 units
		1963	26,236 units
		1964	28,732 units
		1965	13,927 units
		total	161,119 units

Specifications

	220S
Engine type	6 cyl overhead camshaft (M 180)
Bore and stroke	80 x 72.8mm (3.16 x 2.87 in)
Displacement	2195 cc (133.9 cu in)
Power output	110 hp (DIN) @ 5000 rpm (124 hp SAE @ 5200 rpm)
Compression ratio	8.7:1
Torque	17.5 mkg @ 3500 rpm (19.2 mkg 139 ft/lb @ 3700 rpm)
Carburetion	2 dual downdraft carburetors Solex 34 PAJTA from July '63: 35/40 INAT
Engine speed at 100 km/hr	3300 rpm
Gear ratio	I. 3.64:1 automatic I. 3.98:1 II. 2.36:1 (later 2.28:1) II. 2.52:1 III. 1.53:1 III. 1.58:1 IV. 1.00:1 IV. 1.00:1
Rear axle ratio	3.90 4.10
Chassis	unit frame and body
Suspension	independent front, single joint swing axle rear, with coil springs
Brakes and area	drum, 1064 cm^2 (164.9 sq in), servo assisted, optional from Apr. '62 disc, front
Wheelbase	2750mm (108.3 in)
Track, front/rear	1470/1485mm (57.9/58.5 in) from Apr. '62: 1482/1485mm (58.3/58.5 in)
Length	4875mm (191.9 in)
Width	1795mm (70.7 in)
Height	1500mm (59.1 in)
Ground clearance	165mm (6.5 in)
Tires	6.70 x 13 sport; from 1960: 7.25 x 13 sport
Turning circle	12.1-11.9 meters (39 ft)
Steering type and ratio	recirculating ball, 21.4:1 (3.75 turns)
Weight	1345 kg (2959 lbs)
Maximum speed	165 km/hr (103 mph)
Acceleration	15 sec 0-100 km/hr
Fuel consumption	14 liters, super/100 km (16.75 mpg) automatic: 15 liters, super 100km/hr (15.6 mpg)
Fuel tank capatity	65 liters (17.2 gallons)

Prices and Production

The 220SEb four-door sedan sold for . . . . .DM 14,950
    from April 1962 . . . . .DM 15,400
    Power steering . . . . .DM   550
    Hydrak transmission (until 1961) . . . . .DM   450
    Automatic transmission (from August 1961) . . . . .DM 1,400
The 220SEb two-door coupe sold for . . . . .DM 23,500
The 220SEb two-door convertible sold for . . . . .DM 25,500
The price in the United States for the sedan was . . . . .$ 5,187
The price in the United States for the coupe was . . . . .$ 8,895

Production of the 220SEb sedan [111/3] (from August 1959 until
August 1965)

was in	1959	1,579 units
	1960	9,247 units
	1961	10,761 units
	1962	10,786 units
	1963	12,848 units
	1964	14,336 units
	1965	6,529 units
	total	66,086 units

Production of the 220SEb [111/3] coupe and convertible (from September 1960/February 1961 until October 1965)

was in	1960	2 units
	1961	2,537 units
	1962	4,287 units
	1963	3,755 units
	1964	3,528 units
	1965	2,793 units
	total	16,902 units

Model 220SE (1959-1965)

The 220SEb, first shown also in late 1959, was the third of the models to share the identical body style with the others, but was more luxuriously outfitted in its interior.

The fuel-injection engine was essentially the same as that of the previous 220SE model, but now developed 120 horsepower (134 SAE) instead of 115. The maximum speed was 172 kilometers (107 miles) per hour. As in the carbureter engined model, this one had disc brakes on the front wheels fitted from April 1962 and the hydraulic dual braking system available from August 1963 on.

Production of the sedans got under way in August 1959, and in September 1960 a newly styled coupe became available, but it was not produced in quantity until February 1961. The convertible appeared in September 1961. All specifications were the same for the three body styles, except for the weights of the different models. Disc brakes were fitted for the two latter ones from the beginning, and at the same time the dual braking system was available in all three.

The body styles of the convertible and coupe were more modern — the rear fins were eliminated and the edge slightly rounded — and the cars were much more luxuriously equipped. Real leather upholstery was standard and a four-speed automatic transmission with floor-mounted shift lever, as well as a tachometer, were standard equipment of these truly elegant automobiles.

Specifications

	220SEb	220SEb (coupe and convertible)		
Engine type	6 cyl overhead camshaft (M 127)	6 cyl overhead camshaft (M 127)		
Bore and stroke	80 x 72.8mm (3.16 x 2.87 in)	80 x 72.8mm (3.16 x 2.87 in)		
Displacement	2195 cc (133.9 cu in)	2195 cc (133.9 in)		
Power output	120 hp (DIN) @ 4800 rpm (134 hp SAE @ 5000 rpm)	120 hp (DIN) @ 4800 rpm (134 hp SAE @ 5000 rpm)		
Compression ratio	8.7:1	8.7:1		
Torque	19.3 mkg @ 3900 rpm; (21.0 mkg @ 4100 rpm SAE 151.9 ft/lb)			
Fuel injection	Bosch two plunger pump	Bosch two plunger pump		
Engine speed at 100 km/hr	3300 rpm	3300 rpm		
Gear ratios	I. 3.64:1 II. 2.36:1 (later 2.28:1) III. 1.53:1 IV. 1.00:1	I. 3.64:1 II. 2.36:1 (later 2.28:1) III. 1.53:1 IV. 1.00:1	automatic I. II. III. IV.	3.98:1 2.52:1 1.58:1 1.00:1
Rear axle ratio	4.10	4.10		
Chassis	unit frame and body	unit frame and body		
Suspension	independent front, single joint swing axle rear, with coil springs			
Brakes and area	drum, 1064 cm² (164.9 sq in) disc, front; drum, rear servo assisted, optional; from Aug. '63: two circuit hydraulic			
Wheelbase	2750mm (108.3 in)	2750mm (108.3 in)		
Track, front/rear	1470/1485mm (57.9/58.5 in)	1482/1485mm (58.3/58.4 in)		
Length	4875mm (191.9 in)	4880mm (192.1 in)		
Width	1795mm (70.7 in)	1845mm (72.7 in)		
Height	1500mm (59.1 in)	1440mm (57 in)		
Ground clearance	185mm (7.3 in)	185mm (7.3 in)		
Tires	6.70 x 13 sport from 1960: 7.25 x 13 sport	coupe: 7.25 x 13; conv: 750 x 13		
Turning circle	12.1-11.9 meters (39 ft)	12.1-11.9 meters (39 ft)		
Steering type and ratio	recirculating ball, 21.4:1 (3.75 turns) (with servo assistance: 17.3:1; 3.2 turns)	22.7:1 (4.1 turns)		
Weight	1380 kg (3036 lb)	coupe: 1410 kg (3102 lbs); conv: 1510 kg (3322 lbs)		
Maximum speed	172 km/hr (107 mph)	172 km/hr (107 mph)		
Acceleration	14 sec 0-100 km/hr	14 sec 0-100 km/hr		
Fuel consumption	14 liters, super/100 km (16.75 mpg); automatic: 15 liters (15.6 mpg) 14.5 liters/15.5 liters			
Fuel tank capacity	65 liters (17.2 gallons)	65 liter (17.2 gallons)		

Production

Production of the 300SE sedan [112/3] (from April 1961 until July 1965)

was in	1961	13 units
	1962	2,768 units
	1963	995 units
	1964	936 units
	1965	490 units
	total	5,202 units

Production of the 300SE convertible and coupe [112/3] (from February 1962 until December 1967)

was in	1962	331 units
	1963	630 units
	1964	706 units
	1965	710 units
	1966	497 units
	1967	253 units
	total	3,127 units

Production of the 300SE long sedan [112/3] (from December 1962/ March 1963 until August 1965)

was in	1962	1 unit
	1963	387 units
	1964	751 units
	1965	407 units
	total	1,546 units

Model 300SE (1961-1967)

The 300SE was the fourth model to share the new basic body style first shown at the Frankfurt Auto Show in 1959. In appointments it was similar to the 220SE, but it had several important refinements, visible and hidden. The white-wall tires and wider use of chrome trim on the body made it look longer and more elegant than its lesser counterparts, but from afar it seemed the same. An air suspension system and disc brakes on all four wheels were standard. The hydraulic dual braking system was available from August 1963 on.

The 2,996 cubic centimeter light alloy engine with manifold fuel injection developed 160 horsepower at 5,000 revolutions per minute and from January 1964 on, 170 horsepower at 5,400 revolutions per minute. This was achieved by raising the compression ratio from 8.7 to 8.8 to 1; and instead of the two-plunger injection pump, a six-plunger Bosch pump was used. Maximum speeds varied according to rear axle ratios; the 160 horsepower engine with automatic transmission and 3.92 axle produced 175 kilometers per hour, while the 170 horsepower version with manual transmission and 3.75 axle gave the sedan a maximum speed of 200 kilometers (124 miles) per hour.

The 300SE coupe and convertible were added to the line in March 1962, and a longer (2,850 millimeter or 112.2 inch) wheelbase model sedan came out in March 1963.

Prices

The 330SE four-door sedan sold for . . . . .DM	23,100
The 300SE long four-door sedan sold for . . . . .DM	26,400
The 300SE two-door coupe sold for . . . . .DM	31,350
The 300SE two-door convertible sold for. . . . . .DM	33,350
Automatic transmission . . . . .DM	1,400
The price in the United States	
for the sedan in January 1966 was . . . .$	7,980
for the coupe in January 1966 was . . . .$	11,511
for the convertible in January 1966 was. . . . .$	12,295

Specifications

	300SE/ 300SE (long)/ 300SE (coupe and convertible)
Engine type	6 cyl overhead camshaft (M 189)
Bore and stroke	85 x 88mm (3.34 x 3.47 in)
Displacement	2996 cc (182.8 cu in)
Power output	160 hp (DIN) @ 5000 rpm; from Jan. '64: 170 hp (DIN) @ 5400 rpm (185 hp SAE @ 5200 rpm) (195 hp SAE @ 5500 rpm)
Compression ratio	8.7:1 from Jan. '64: 8.8:1
Torque	25.6 mkg @ 3800 rpm 25.4 mkg @ 4000 rpm (28.3 mkg @ 4000 rpm SAE 204.5 ft/lb)
Fuel injection	Bosch two plunger pump; from Jan. '64: six plunger pump
Engine speed at 100 km/hr	3310 rpm
Gear ratios	I. 4.05:1 automatic I. 3.98:1 (16.3) II. 2.28:1 II. 2.52:1 (10.3) III. 1.53:1 III. 1.58:1 (6.47) IV. 1.00:1 IV. 1.00:1 (4.10)
Rear axle ratio	3.92 or 3.75 4.10 from 1963: 3.92 or 3.75
Chassis	unit frame and body
Suspension	independent front and rear, with coil springs, single joint swing axle, air suspension
Brakes and area	disc, 253/255mm (99.6/100.4), servo assisted, two circuit hydraulic
Wheelbase	2750mm (108.3 in); SE long: 2850mm (112.2 in)
Track, front/rear	1482/1490mm (58.3/58.6)
Length	4875mm (191.9 in); long: 5875mm (231.2 in); coupe & convertible: 4880mm (192.1 in)
Width	1795mm (70.7 in) coupe & convertible: 1845mm (72.6 in)
Height	1455mm (58 in) coupe: 1395mm; conv: 1400mm (55.1 in)
Ground clearance	185mm (7.3 in)
Tires	7.50 x 13
Turning circle	12.1-11.9 meters (39 ft); long: 12.4-12.2 meters (40 ft)
Steering type and ratio	recirculating ball, 17.3:1 (3.2 turns), servo assisted
Weight	1580 kg (3476 lbs); long: 1630 kg (3586 lbs); coupe: 1600 kg (3520 lbs); conv: 1700 kg (3740 lbs)
Maximum speed	160 hp manual, 3.92 axle 180 km/hr (112 mph); autom. 175 km/hr 170 hp manual, 3.92 axle 190 km/hr (118 mph); autom. 185 km/hr 170 hp manual, 3.75 axle 200 km/hr (124 pmh); autom. 195 km/hr
Acceleration	160 hp: 13 sec 0-100 km/hr; 170 hp: 12 sec 0-100 km/hr
Fuel consumption	17 liters, super/100 km (13.7 mpg); automatic: 19 liters (12.3 mpg)
Fuel tank capacity	65 liters (17.2 gallons); from Jan. '63: 82 liters (21.6 gallons)

51

Prices and Production

The 230SL roadster sold in 1963 for . . . . DM 20,600
    from April 1966 for . . . . .DM 21,100
The 230SL coupe sold in 1963 for . . . . .DM 20,950
    from April 1966 for . . . . .DM 21,450
    Hard top (for the roadster) . . . . .DM 1,100
    Power steering . . . . .DM   550
    Automatic transmission . . . . .DM 1,400
Prices in the United States were, in April 1966,
    for the 230SL roadster (East coast) . . . .$ 6,185
    (West coast) . . . .$ 6,262
    for the 230SL coupe (East coast) . . . .$ 6,343
    (West coast) . . . .$ 6,420
    for the 230SL coupe/roadster (East coast) . . . .$ 6,587
    (West coast) . . . .$ 6,665
    Power steering (April 1966) . . . .$ 171
    Automatic transmission . . . .$ 342
Prices previously were for the roadster . . . .$ 6,144
    for the coupe . . . .$ 6,301
    for the coupe/roadster . . . .$ 6,543

Production of the 230SL [113] (from March/July 1963 until
January 1967)

	was in	1963	1,465 units
		1964	6,911 units
		1965	6,325 units
		1966	4,945 units
		1967	185 units
		total	19,831 units

Model 230SL (1963-1967)

The 230SL sports car was first introduced at the Geneva Auto Show in March 1963. It was the successor to the 190SL which was phased out in February of that year. The engine for the 230SL was an enlarged version of the 220SE power unit, displacing 2,306 cubic centimeters and developing 150 horsepower (170 SAE) at 5,500 (5,600) revolutions per minute. Compression ratio was 9.3 to 1. The fuel was injected into the intake duct in the cylinder head instead of into the intake suction pipe as in the other models.

The four-speed transmission lever was placed on the floor and an automatic transmission was available. The rear axle ratio was 3.75 to 1. Maximum speeds were for the manual transmission 200 kilometers (124.2 miles) per hour and using the automatic transmission, 195 kilometers (121.2 miles) per hour.

A two-circuit servo brake system was installed as well as a vacuum operated brake booster. Disc brakes were fitted in front and drum brakes on the rear wheels. The coupe version had a slightly converse top, giving it the appearance of a pagoda top. The large glass area afforded an excellent view for the driver in all directions.

To start the introduction of the new model off with an impressive event, Eugen Böhringer won the tortuous Spa-Sofia-Liege Rally, driving the new 230SL. It was a spectacular performance for driver and car to win this initial test against strong international competition.

Specifications

	230SL
Engine type	6 cyl overhead camshaft (M 127)
Bore and stroke	82 x 72.8mm (3.23 x 2.87 in)
Displacement	2,306 cc (140.7 cu in)
Power output	150 hp (DIN) @ 5500 rpm (170 hp SAE @ 5600 rpm)
Compression ratio	9.3:1
Torque	20 mkg @ 4200 rpm (22 mkg @ 4500 rpm 159 ft/lbs)
Fuel injection	Bosch six plunger pump
Engine speed at 100 km/hr	3145 rpm
Gear ratios	until 1965 automatic: I. 4.42:1 (later 4.05) I. 3.98:1 (14.9) II. 2.28:1 (later 2.23) II. 2.52:1 (9.45) III. 1.53:1 (later 1.42) III. 1.58:1 (5.92) IV. 1.00:1 (later 1.00) IV. 1.00:1 (3.75)
Rear axle ratio	3.75; from Sept. '65: 3.69 or 3.92
Chassis	unit frame and body
Suspension	independent front, single joint swing axle rear, with coil springs
Brakes and area	disc, front; drum, rear, servo assist, two circuit hydraulic, 253/230mm (9.96/9.06 in)
Wheelbase	2400mm (94.5 in)
Track, front/rear	1486/1487mm (58.5/58.5 in)
Length	4285mm (168.8 in)
Width	1760mm (69.2 in)
Height	1305mm (51.4 in)
Ground clearance	139mm (5.5 in)
Tires	185 HR 14 radial
Turning circle	10.5 meters (34 ft)
Steering type and ratio	recirculating ball, 22.7:1 (4.1 turns); servo assisted 17.3:1 (3.2 turns)
Weight	roadster: 1300 kg (2860 lbs); coupe: 1380 kg (3036 lbs)
Maximum speed	200 km/hr (124 mph); automatic: 195 km/hr (121 mph)
Acceleration	11 sec 0-100 km/hr; automatic: 13 sec 0-100 km/hr
Fuel consumption	14 liter, super/100 km (16.75 mpg)
Fuel tank capacity	65 liters (17.2 gallons)

Model 250SL (1966-1968)

The 250SL model made its brief appearance toward the end of 1966. The first few cars (seventeen units) were built in late November and in December of that year. The body was the same as that of the former 230SL which it replaced. Minor improvements had been made in the interior furnishings and outfitting, such as a pressure-absorbing steering wheel, better seat belts, and modified lighting of some instruments, but basically it was the same.

With the larger engine of 2,496 cubic centimeter (152.3 cubic inch) displacement and 150 horsepower (DIN) and 170 SAE, and especially vastly increased torque from the former 159 ft/lbs. to 173.6 ft/lbs. (both at 4,500 revolutions per minute), this new model showed an appreciable improvement in performance. Fitted with the four- or five-speed transmission and a rear axle ratio of 3.69, the car reached 19.7 miles at 1,000 revolutions per minute in top gear — the same as that of the 230SL model, but it was much more responsive. The gear ratios of the later production of the former model were maintained. Along with the engine of the 250SE line, the sports car also got the disc brakes, front and rear, resulting in some improvement in stopping the car; power assist was standard.

The 250SL was actually a one-year production car. It was soon to be replaced by a yet larger engined model and was produced in any quantity only during the year 1967. Only two cars were built in 1968.

Prices and Production

The 250SL coupe sold in 1967 for . . . . .DM 22,800
    Power steering . . . . .DM   550
    Automatic transmission .DM 1,400
The 250SL roadster sold in the U.S. in September 1967
    (East coast) for. . . . .$ 6,485
    (West coast) for. . . . .$ 6,568
The 250SL coupe sold (East coast) for . . . .$ 6,647
The 250SL coupe/roadster sold (East coast) for . . . . . .$ 6,897

Production of the 250SL [113 A] (from November/December 1966 until January 1968)

	was in 1966	17 units
	1967	5,177 units
	1968	2 units
	total	5,196 units

Specifications

	250SL
Engine type	6 cyl overhead camshaft (M 129)
Bore and stroke	82 x 78.8mm (3.23 x 3.1 in)
Displacement	2496 cc (152.3 cu in)
Power output	150 hp (DIN) @ 5500 rpm (170 hp SAE @ 5600 rpm)
Compression ratio	9.3:1
Torque	22 mkg @ 4200 rpm (24 mkg SAE @ 4500 rpm 173.6 ft/lb)
Fuel injection	Bosch six plunger pump
Engine speed at 100 km/hr	3245 rpm
Gear ratios	I. 4.05:1 automatic I. 3.98:1 II. 2.23:1 II. 2.52:1 III. 1.42:1 III. 1.58:1 IV. 1.00:1 IV. 1.00:1
Rear axle ratio	3.69
Chassis	unit frame and body
Suspension	independent front and rear, with coil springs, single joint swing axle
Brakes and area	disc, servo assist, two circuit hydraulic, 273/279mm (10.75/10.99 in)
Wheelbase	2400mm (94.5 in)
Track, front/rear	1486/1487mm (58.5/58.5 in)
Length	4285mm (168.8 in)
Width	1760mm (69.2 in)
Height	1305mm (51.4 in)
Ground clearance	139mm (5.5 in)
Tires	185 H 14 radial
Turning circle	10.5 meters (34 ft)
Steering type and ratio	recirculating ball, 22.7:1 (4.1 turns); servo assisted, 17. 3:1 (3.2 turns)
Weight	roadster: 1300 kg (2860 lbs); coupe: 1380 kg (3036 lbs)
Maximum speed	200 km/hr (124 mph); automatic: 195 km/hr (121 mph)
Acceleration	11 sec 0-100 km/hr; automatic: 13 sec 0-100 km/hr
Fuel consumption	14 liters, super/100 km (16.75 mpg)
Fuel tank capacity	82 liters (21.7 gallons)

Prices

The 280SL sports coupe/roadster sold for ....DM 23,793
    Power steering ....DM 550
    Automatic Transmission...............DM 1,400
Prices were in March 1968 (East coast)
    for the 280SL roadster......................$ 6,485
    coupe ....$ 6,647
    roadster/coupe ....$ 6,897
Prices were in March 1968 (West coast)
    for the 280SL roadster......................$ 6,585
    coupe ....$ 6,731
    roadster/coupe ....$ 6,981
Prices were in September 1968 (East coast)
    for the 280SL roadster......................$ 6,638
    coupe ....$ 6,800
    roadster/coupe ....$ 7,050
Prices were in October 1969 (East coast)
    for the 280SL roadster......................$ 6,952
    coupe ....$ 7,118
    roadster/coupe ....$ 7,374
Prices were in October 1970 (East coast)
    for the 280SL roadster......................$ 7,444
    coupe ....$ 7,617
    roadster/coupe ....$ 7,884
Prices were in March 1971 (East coast)
    for the 280SL roadster......................$ 7,469
    coupe ....$ 7,642
    roadster/coupe ....$ 7,909
    Power steering (October 1970)...............$ 198
    Automatic transmission ....$ 392

Model 280SL (1967-1971)

The 280SL sports car was the next, and last, graduation in the development of the particular model line. Begun in March 1963 as the 230SL, it had succeeded the popular 190SL of which nearly 26,000 units were produced. Yet in the three variations (230SL, 250SL, and 280SL) this model sold almost twice as many cars. It was not a competitive, but luxurious, fast touring sports car.

The six-cylinder 2,778 cubic centimeter displacement engine for the 280SL was entirely new. It retained the same design characteristics as the 250 engine, with single overhead camshaft and a seven main bearing crankshaft. An air cooler for the lubricating oil, similar to that employed on racing cars, replaced the oil-water heat exchanger of the previous engine design. Developing 180 SAE horsepower (up from 170) and 193 ft/lbs. torque (up from 174), the performance of this newest model sports car was tremendously enhanced, despite the restricting stricter emission controls. (The horsepower per liter ratio was for the 230SL/74, 250SL/68, and 280SL/65.)

For the American market a rear axle ratio of 4.08 was furnished, but the other two ratios, 3.92 and 3.69, were available upon special request. As on the two previous models, the five-speed manual gearbox was also available, while the four-speed one was standard. Power steering was not yet a standard item on the car. The 280SL was offered as a coupe, roadster, or combination roadster-coupe model.

Production

Production of the 280SL [113 E28] (from November 1967/January 1968 until March 1971)

was in	1967	143 units
	1968	6,930 units
	1969	8,047 units
	1970	7,935 units
	1971	830 units
	total	23,885 units

Specifications

	280SL
Engine type	6 cyl overhead camshaft (M 130)
Bore and stroke	86.5 x 78.8mm (3.41 x 3.10 in)
Displacement	2778 cc (169.5 cu in)
Power output	170 hp (DIN) @ 5700 rpm (180 SAE hp @ 5700 rpm) or 180 hp (DIN) @ 5900 rpm, but not for U.S.
Compression ratio	9.5:1
Torque	24.5 mkg @ 4250 rpm (26.7 mkg SAE @ 4500 rpm 193 ft/lb)
Fuel injection	Bosch six plunger pump
Engine speed at 100 km/hr	3500 rpm
Gear ratios	I. 4.05:1 automatic I. 3.98:1 (16.21) II. 2.23:1 II. 2.52:1 (10.27) III. 1.42:1 III. 1.58:1 (6.44) IV. 1.00:1 IV. 1.00:1 (4.08)
Rear axle ratio	4.08 upon request: 3.92, 3.69
Chassis	unit frame and body
Suspension	independent front and rear, with coil springs, single joint swing axle
Brakes and area	disc, servo assist, two circuit hydraulic, 273/279mm (10.75/10.99 in)
Wheelbase	2400mm (94.5 in)
Track, front/rear	1486/1487mm (58.5/58.5 in)
Length	4285mm (168.8 in)
Width	1760mm (69.2 in)
Height	1305mm (51.4 in)
Ground clearance	139mm (5.5 in)
Tires	185 H 14 radial
Turning circle	10.5 meters (34 ft)
Steering type	recirculating ball, servo assisted 17.2:1 (3.2 turns)
Weight	roadster: 1340 kg (2948 lbs); coupe: 1420 kg (3124 lbs)
Maximum speed	195 km/hr (121 mph); automatic: 190 km/hr (118 pmh)
Acceleration	10 sec 0-100 km/hr; automatic: 11 sec 0-100 km/hr
Fuel consumption	14 liters, super/100 km (16.75 mpg)
Fuel tank capacity	82 liters (21.7 gallons)

Prices

The 600 four-door limousine sold for . . . . .DM 56,500

The 600 four-door pullman sold for . . . . .DM 63,500

In the United States, advertised in May 1964,
prices were for the limousine (called
5-passenger sedan) . . . .$ 19,500
and for the pullman (called
7-passenger sedan) . . . .$ 24,000

The price list of October 1965 offered the
limousine (East coast) for . . . .$ 20,143
(West coast) for. . . . .$ 20,291
pullman (East coast) for . . . .$ 23,098
(West coast) for . . . .$ 23,245

The price list of October 1970 (registration 1971 vehicles)
offered the limousine (East coast) for . . . .$ 25,707
(West coast) for. . . . .$ 25,920
pullman (East coast) for . . . .$ 29,385
(West coast) for. . . . .$ 29,617

The price list of December 1971 (registration 1972 vehicles)
offered the limousine (East coast) for . . . .$ 32,695
pullman (East coast) for . . . .$ 37,928

Other prices were, in September 1966 (East coast)
limousine. . . . .$ 22,299
pullman. . . . .$ 25,582

in September 1968 (East coast)
limousine. . . . .$ 23,007
pullman. . . . .$ 26,290

in October 1969 (East coast)
limousine. . . . .$ 23,580
pullman. . . . .$ 26,953

Model 600 (1963-   )

The 600 model — the Grosser Mercedes — was introduced at the Frankfurt Auto Show in 1963. It restored the tradition of sumptuous luxury and ultimate prestige of Mercedes-Benz.

A new V-type eight-cylinder engine of 6.3 liters (6,329 cubic centimeters) developing 250 horsepower (300 SAE) powered this newest edition of the great Mercedes to a maximum speed of 205 kilometers (127 miles) per hour. The 600 model was available in two body styles: a 5/6-seat limousine or 7/8-passenger pullman with wheelbases of 3,200 millimeters (126 inches) and 3,900 millimeters (153.5 inches), respectively. Overall length was 218 and 246 inches. From 1965 on, a landaulet also became available.

This fine automobile incorporated all modern design elements: fuel injection, overhead camshaft engine, air suspension and shock absorbers adjustment, disc brakes on all four wheels, automatic four-speed transmission and power steering, central vacuum locking system for the doors and luggage compartment, adjustable steering wheel, and two separate heating and ventilating systems. It was truly a majestic car of the highest order and an honorable descendant of the distinctive Great Mercedes automobiles of former years.

That year, 1963, the company offered fourteen passenger car models for sale. However, not all of them were made available to the American public, and most of them were naturally not entirely new models.

Production

Production of the 600 and 600 long model [100]
(from August 1963/September 1964)

		Limousine	Pullman
was in	1963	2 units	1 unit
	1964	99 units	8 units
	1965	345 units	63 units
	1966	293 units	30 units
	1967	138 units	21 units
	1968	184 units	39 units
	1969	279 units	57 units
	1970	198 units	38 units
	1971	186 units	51 units
	1972	172 units	38 units
	1973	64 units	18 units
	1974	24 units	28 units
	1975	25 units	17 units
	total	2,009 units	409 units

Specifications

	600	Pullman
Engine type	V-8 cyl overhead camshaft, one for each bank (M 100)	
Bore and stroke	103 x 95mm (4.06 x 3.74 in)	103 x 95mm (4.06 x 3.74 in)
Displacement	6332 cc (386.3 cu in)	6332 cc (386.3 cu in)
Power output	250 hp (DIN) @ 4000 rpm (300 hp SAE @ 4100 rpm)	
Compression ratio	9.0:1	9.0:1
Torque	51 mkg @ 2800 rpm (434 ft/lbs @ 3000 rpm)	
Fuel injection	Bosch eight plunger pump	Bosch eight plunger pump
Engine speed at 100 km/hr	2475 rpm	2475 rpm
Gear ratios	I. 3.98:1 (12.86) II. 2.52:1 (8.14) III. 1.58:1 (5.10) IV. 1.00:1 (3.23)	I. 3.98:1 (12.86) II. 2.52:1 (8.14) (later 2.46:1) III. 1.58:1 (5.10) IV. 1.00:1 (3.23)
Rear axle ratio	3.23	3.23
Chassis	unit frame and body	unit frame and body
Suspension	independent front, single joint swing axle rear, air suspension	
Brakes and area	discs, 291/294.5mm (114.6/115.9 in), servo assisted, two circuit hydraulic	
Wheelbase	3200mm (126 in)	3900mm (153.5 in)
Track, front/rear	1587/1581mm (62.5/62 in)	1587/1581mm (62.5/62 in)
Length	5540mm (218 in)	6240mm (246 in)
Width	1950mm (76.8 in)	1950mm (76.8 in)
Height	1500mm (59.5 in)	1510mm (59.5 in)
Ground clearance	200mm (7.9 in) (later: 152mm (6.0 in)	
Tires	9.00 x 15 super sport	9.00 x 15 super sport
Turning circle	12.4 meters (40.7 ft) (later: 12.7m)	14.6 meters (47.8 ft) (later: 15.0m)
Steering type and ratio	recirculating ball, servo assisted, 17.3:1 (3.3 turns)	
Weight	2470 kg (5434 lbs) (later: 2475 kg)	2640 kg (5808 lbs) (later: 2660 kg)
Maximum speed	205 km/hr (127 mph)	200 km/hr (124 mph)
Acceleration	10 sec 0-100 km/hr (later: 9.7 sec)	12 sec 0-100 km/hr
Fuel consumption	24 liters, super/100 km (10.2 mpg)	26 liters, super/100 km (9 mpg)
Fuel tank capacity	112 liters (30 gallons)	112 liters (30 gallons)

Prices and Production

The 200 four-door sedan sold for . . . . .DM 10,800
    from April 1966 for. . . . . .DM 11,000
    Power steering . . . . .DM   500
    Automatic transmission .DM 1,400
The price in the United States was in 1965
    (East coast) . . . .$ 3,929
      (West coast) . . . .$ 4,039
    in September 1966 (East coast) . . . .$ 4,084
    in September 1967 (East coast) . . . .$ 4,179
    Power steering (1965) . . . .$ 171
    Automatic transmission . . . .$ 342

Production of the 200 model [110] (from July 1965 until February 1968)

	was in 1965	16,864 units
	1966	26,842 units
	1967	26,169 units
	1968	332 units
	total	70,207 units

Model 200 (1965-1968)

The 200 model was first shown, together with four other new models, at the Frankfurt Auto Show in 1965. It used the same body as the former 190c sedan which it replaced. Outwardly the change was a relocation of the indicator lights from the cowl to the front, just below the headlights, a redesigned cluster of rear lights, and a narrow chrome strip at the rear window for the air ventilation exit.

The four-cylinder engine had been increased from 1.9 liters to 2 liters (1,988 cubic centimeters) and developed 95 horsepower (105 SAE) instead of the former 80 horsepower (90 SAE). A five-bearing crankshaft gave it smoother and quieter operation. With the same weight as previously, performance was improved by some 20 percent. Acceleration figures from 0 to 100 kilometers (62 miles) were 15 seconds and maximum speed was 161 kilometers (100 miles) per hour. The 200 sedan was the smallest of the seventeen different models of passenger cars the company offered that year.

Specifications

	200
Engine type	4 cyl overhead camshaft (M 121)
Bore and stroke	87 x 83.6mm (3.43 x 3.29 in)
Displacement	1988 cc (121.27 cu in)
Power output	95 hp (DIN) @ 5200 rpm (105 hp SAE @ 5400 rpm)
Compression ratio	9.0:1
Torque	15.7 mkg @ 3600 rpm (16.9 mkg @ 3800 rpm 122.3 ft/lb)
Carburetion	2 downdraft carburetors Solex 38 PDSJ
Engine speed at 100 km/hr	3310 rpm
Gear ratios	I. 4.09:1 automatic I. 3.98:1 II. 2.25:1 II. 2.52:1 III. 1.42:1 III. 1.58:1 IV. 1.00:1 IV. 1.00:1
Rear axle ratio	4.08
Chassis	unit frame and body
Suspension	independent front, single joint swing axle rear, with coil springs
Brakes and area	disc, front; drum, rear; servo assist, two circuit hydraulic, 253/230mm (9.96/9.06 in)
Wheelbase	2700mm (106.3 in)
Track, front/rear	1482/1485mm (58.3/58.5 in)
Length	4730mm (186.5 in)
Width	1795mm (70.7 in)
Height	1495mm (58.8 in)
Ground clearance	185mm (7.3 in)
Tires	7.00 x 13
Turning circle	11.8-11.6 meters (39 ft)
Steering type and ratio	recirculating ball, 22.7:1 (4.1 turns); servo assisted 17.3:1 (3.2 turns)
Weight	1275 kg (2805 lbs)
Maximum speed	161 km/hr (100 mph); automatic: 158 km/hr (98 mph)
Acceleration	15 sec 0-100 km/hr; automatic: 16 sec 0-100 km/hr
Fuel consumption	12.5 liters, super/100 km (18.75 mpg); automatic: 13.5 liters, super (17.4 mpg)
Fuel tank capacity	65 liters (17.2 gallons)

Model 200D (1965-1968)

The 200D was another new car, introduced at the time of the Frankfurt Show in 1965. As always, this diesel-engined model shared all of the appointments with the gasoline-engined model in its category. The body was exactly the same, and it, too, replaced the former 190Dc. Unlike its companion car, the engine of the 200D was of the same displacement as the previous one which already had displaced 1,988 cubic centimeters.

A five-bearing crankshaft, along with other noise attenuating measures, were built into the engine for quieter and smoother operation and less fatigue to the driver. These design features released greater power and increased the maximum speed of the car to 130 kilometers (80.8 miles) per hour. Fuel consumption remained extremely moderate, averaging between 7 to 9 liters (31 to 40 gallons) at regular cruising speeds. The standard consumption, according to DIN, was 35 miles per gallon (8.1 liters per 100 kilometers) at 60 miles per hour.

Since 1936, some 500,000 diesel-engined Mercedes-Benz cars had been built, attesting to the popularity of these economic and robust automobiles.

Prices and Production

The 200D four-door sedan sold for	.DM	11,300
from April 1966 for	.DM	11,500
Power steering	.DM	500
Automatic transmission	.DM	1,400
The price in the United States was in 1965		
(East coast)	.$	4,142
(West coast)	.$	4,252
in September 1966 (East coast)	.$	4,305
in September 1967 (East coast)	.$	4,380
Power steering (1965)	.$	171
Automatic transmission	.$	342

Production of the 200D model [110] (from July 1965 until February 1968)

was in	1965	30,937 units
	1966	61,707 units
	1967	68,399 units
	1968	575 units
	total	161,618 units

Specifications

	200D
Engine type	4 cyl diesel, overhead camshaft (OM 621)
Bore and stroke	87 x 83.6mm (3.43 x 3.29 in)
Displacement	1988 cc (121.27 cu in)
Power output	55 hp (DIN) @ 4200 rpm (60 hp SAE)
Compression ratio	21:1
Torque	11.5 mkg @ 2400 rpm (12 mkg SAE 87 ft/lbs)
Fuel injection	Bosch injection pump
Engine speed at 100 km/hr	3300 rpm
Gear ratios	I. 4.09:1 automatic I. 3.98:1 II. 2.25:1 II. 2.52:1 III. 1.42:1 III. 1.58:1 IV. 1.00:1 IV. 1.00:1
Rear axle ratio	3.92
Chassis	unit frame and body
Suspension	independent front, single joint swing axle rear, with coil springs air suspension, optional
Brakes and area	disc front; drum, rear, servo assist, 253/230mm (9.96/9.06 in) two circuit hydraulic
Wheelbase	2700mm (106.3 in)
Track, front/rear	1482/1485mm (58.3/58.5 in)
Length	4730mm (186.5 in)
Width	1795mm (70.7 in)
Height	1495mm (58.8 in)
Ground clearance	185mm (7.3 in)
Tires	7.00 x 13
Turning circle	11.8-11.6 meters (39 ft)
Steering type and ratio	recirculating ball, 22.7:1 (4.1 turns); servo assisted 17.3:1 (3.2 turns)
Weight	1325 kg (2915 lbs)
Maximum speed	130 km/hr (81 mph)
Acceleration	29 sec 0-100 km/hr; automatic: 30 sec 0-100 km/hr
Fuel consumption	9 liters/100 km (26 mpg); automatic: 10 liter/100 km (23 mpg)
Fuel tank capacity	65 liters (17.2 gallons)

Model 230 (1965-1968)

The 230 model, also first shown at the Frankfurt Show in 1965, was the successer to the 220 model. The body style was the same as that of the 200 line introduced at the same time. However, with the six-cylinder engine this model combined the compact dimensions with the performance and efficiency of a modern six-cylinder car.

The new engine had a bore of 82 millimeters, instead of the 80 millimeters of the former 2,195 cubic centimeter engine, resulting in an increase to 2,281 cubic centimeters (139.2 cubic inches). With a compression ratio of 9 to 1 and the new camshaft, the engine developed 105 horsepower at 5,200 revolutions per minute or 118 SAE horsepower at 5,400 revolutions per minute. The weight of this six-cylinder engine, now with a seven main bearing crankshaft for greater smoothness, was but slightly more than that of the four-cylinder unit and resulted in greatly improved performance over that model. Maximum speed was increased to 168 kilometers (104 miles) per hour. Automatic transmission and power steering were optional items for this model, of course.

Prices and Production

The 230 four-door sedan sold for . . . . .DM 11,700
    from April 1966 for. . . . . .DM 11,950
    Power steering . . . . .DM   500
    Automatic transmission .DM 1,400
The price in the United States was in 1965
    (East coast) . . . .$ 4,113
        (West coast) . . . .$ 4,223
    in September 1966 (East coast) . . . .$ 4,280
    in September 1967 (East coast) . . . .$ 4,405
    Power steering (1956) . . . .$ 171
    Automatic transmission . . . .$ 342

Production of the 230 model [110] (from July 1965 until February 1968)

was in	1965	8,548 units
	1966	14,951 units
	1967	16,441 units
	1968	318 units
	total	40,258 units

Specifications

	230
Engine type	6 cyl overhead camshaft (M 180)
Bore and stroke	82 x 72.8mm (3.23 x 2.87 in)
Displacement	2281 cc (139.2 cu in)
Power output	105 hp (DIN) @ 5200 rpm (118 hp SAE @ 5400 rpm)
Compression ratio	9:1
Torque	17.7 mkg @ 3600 rpm (19 mkg SAE @ 3800 rpm 137.4 ft/lb)
Carburetion	2 downdraft carburetors Solex 38 PDSJ
Engine speed at 100 km/hr	3470 rpm
Gear ratios	I. 4.09:1 automatic I. 3.98:1 II. 2.25:1 II. 2.52:1 III. 1.42:1 III. 1.58:1 IV. 1.00:1 IV. 1.00:1
Rear axle ratio	4.08
Chassis	unit frame and body
Suspension	independent front, single joint swing axle rear, with coil springs air suspension, optional
Brakes and area	disc front; drum rear, servo assist, two circuit hydraulic, 253/230mm (9.96/9.06 in)
Wheelbase	2700mm (106.3 in)
Track, front/rear	1482/1485mm (58.3/58.5 in)
Length	4730mm (186.5 in)
Width	1795mm (70.7 in)
Height	1495mm (58.8 in)
Ground clearance	185mm (7.3 in)
Tires	7.00 S 13
Turning circle	11.8-11.6 meters (39 ft)
Steering type and ratio	recirculating ball, 22.7:1 (4.1 turns); servo assisted 17.3:1 (3.2 turns)
Weight	1305 kg (2871 lbs)
Maximum speed	168 km/hr (104 mph); automatic: 165 km/hr (103 mph)
Acceleration	14 sec 0-100 km/hr; automatic: 16 sec 0-100 km/hr
Fuel consumption	15 liters, super/100 km (15.6 mpg); automatic: 16 liters, super (14.7 mpg)
Fuel tank capacity	65 liters (17.2 gallons)

Model 230S (1965-1968)

The 230S model differed only slightly from the 230 model with which it was first shown at the Frankfurt Show in 1965. The body was practically identical except in the arrangement of the headlights which were combined into one large covered unit. The car replaced the former 220S model and was now the top model of the new class series of passenger cars.

The six-cylinder engine with overhead camshaft had two two-phase downdraft carburetors with automatic starting device. The valve timing permitted a maxium engine speed of 6,250 revolutions per minute without any risk. The horsepower output of the 2,281 cubic centimeter displacement engine was 120 horsepower at 5,400 revolutions per minute (or 135 SAE at 5,600), the same as that of the former 220S model. Compression ratio was 9 to 1. Maximum speed was given at 176 kilometers (110 miles) per hour, and in third gear a top speed of 125 kilometers (78 miles) per hour could be achieved.

Prices and Production

The 230S four-door sedan sold for . . . . .DM 13,750
    from April 1966 for. . . . . .DM 14,000
    Power steering . . . . .DM   500
    Automatic transmission .DM 1,400
The price in the United States was in 1965
    (East coast) . . . .$ 4,754
    (West coast) . . . .$ 4,869
    in September 1966 (East coast) . . . .$ 4,910
    in September 1967 (East coast) . . . .$ 5,035
    Power steering (1965) . . . .$ 171
    Automatic transmission . . . .$ 342

Production of the 230S model [111/1A] (from July 1965 until January 1968)

	was in	1965	12,621 units
		1966	17,230 units
		1967	11,176 units
		1968	80 units
		total	41,107 units

Specifications

	230S
Engine type	6 cyl overhead camshaft (M 180)
Bore and stroke	82 x 72.8mm (3.23 x 2.87 in)
Displacement	2281 cc (139.2 cu in)
Power output	120 hp (DIN) @ 5400 rpm (135 hp SAE @ 5600 rpm)
Compression ratio	9:1
Torque	18.2 mkg @ 4200 rpm (20 mkg SAE 144.7 ft/lb)
Carburetion	2 dual downdraft carburetors Zenith 35/40 INAT
Engine speed at 100 km/hr	3415 rpm
Gear ratios	I. 4.05:1 automatic I. 3.98:1 II. 2.23:1 II. 2.52:1 III. 1.42:1 III. 1.58:1 IV. 1.00:1 IV. 1.00:1
Rear axle ratio	4.08
Chassis	unit frame and body
Suspension	independent front, single joint swing axle rear, with coil springs, air suspension
Brakes and area	disc front; drum rear, servo assist, two circuit hydraulic, 253/230mm (9.96/9.06 in)
Wheelbase	2750mm (108.2 in)
Track, front/rear	1482/1485mm (58.3/58.5 in)
Length	4730mm (186.5 in)
Width	1795mm (70.7 in)
Height	1495mm (58.8 in)
Ground clearance	185mm (7.3 in)
Tires	7.25 x 13
Turning circle	12.0-11.8 meters (39 ft)
Steering type and ratio	recirculating ball, 22.7:1 (4.1 turns); servo assisted, 17.3:1 (3.2 turns)
Weight	1350 kg (2970 lbs)
Maximum speed	176 km/hr (109 mph); automatic: 174 km/hr (108 mph)
Acceleration	13 sec 0-100 km/hr; automatic: 15 sec 0-100 km/hr
Fuel consumption	15 liters, super/100 km (15.6 mpg); automatic: 16 liters, super (14.7 mpg)
Fuel tank capacity	65 liters (17.2 gallons)

Prices and Production

The 250S four-door sedan sold for . . . . .DM 15,300
    from April 1966 for. .DM 15,800
    Power steering . . . . .DM   550
    Automatic transmission . . . . .DM 1,400
The price in the United States was in 1965
    (East coast) . . . .$ 5,696
    (West coast) . . . .$ 5,806
    in September 1966 (East coast) . . . .$ 5,747
    in September 1967 (East coast) . . . .$ 5,897
    Power steering (1965) . . . .$ 171
    Automatic transmission . . . .$ 342

Production of the 250S model [108 II] (from July/September
1965 until March 1969)

	was in	1965	2,844 units
		1966	31,564 units
		1967	37,866 units
		1968	2,014 units
		1969	389 units
		total	74,677 units

Model 250S (1965-1969)

The 250S model, also first shown at Frankfurt in 1965, had a brand new body style. The tail fins had been entirely eliminated and the overall appearance was similar to that of the coupe models. The body waist line was lowered and window area increased, with the windshield being 17 percent larger than that of the 220S model. The flat roof made it look wider, but width had increased by only 15 millimeters (0.59 inches). Height was reduced by 60 millimeters (2.36 inches).

The 2,496 cubic centimeter (152.3 cubic inch) engine was developed from the 2.2-liter power unit, but it had a larger bore and stroke and a seven-bearing crankshaft. A higher compression ratio and larger valves and induction passages were other changes. A double exhaust pipe was standard. The engine developed 130 horsepower at 5,400 revolutions per minute or 146 SAE horsepower at 5,600 revolutions.

Maximum speed of the 250S sedan was given as 180 kilometers (112 miles) per hour, and maximum allowable engine speed was 6,300 revolutions per minute.

Specifications

	250S				
Engine type	6 cyl overhead camshaft (M 108)				
Bore and stroke	82 x 78.8mm (3.23 x 3.1 in)				
Displacement	2496 cc (152.3 cu in)				
Power output	130 hp (DIN) @ 5400 rpm (146 hp SAE @ 5600 rpm)				
Compression ratio	9:1				
Torque	19.8 mkg @ 4000 rpm (21.75 mkg SAE @ 4200 rpm 157.3 ft/lb)				
Carburetion	2 dual downdraft carburetors Zenith 35/40 INAT				
Engine speed at 100 km/hr	3245 rpm				
Gear ratios	I.	4.05:1	automatic I.	3.98:1	(15.6)
	II.	2.23:1	II.	2.52:1	(9.88)
	III.	1.42:1	III.	1.58:1	(6.19)
	IV.	1.00:1	IV.	1.00:1	(3.92)
Rear axle ratio	3.92				
Chassis	unit frame and body				
Suspension	independent front, single joint swing axle rear, with coil springs, air suspension standard				
Brakes and area	disc, servo assist, two circuit hydraulic, 273/279mm (10.75/10.99 in)				
Wheelbase	2750mm (108.3 in)				
Track, front/rear	1482/1485mm (58.3/58.5 in)				
Length	4900mm (192.9 in)				
Width	1810mm (71.3 in)				
Height	1440mm (56.7 in)				
Ground clearance	145mm (5.7 in)				
Tires	7.35 H 14 or 185 H 14				
Turning circle	12.1-11.9 meters (39 ft)				
Steering type and ratio	recirculating ball, 22.7:1 (4.1 turns); servo assisted 17.3:1 (3.2 turns)				
Weight	1440 kg (3168 lbs)				
Maximum speed	182 km/hr (113 mph); automatic: 177 km/hr (110 mph)				
Acceleration	13 sec 0-100 km/hr; automatic: 14 sec 0-100 km/hr				
Fuel consumption	16 liters, super/100 km (14.7 mpg); automatic: 17 liters, super (13.7 mpg)				
Fuel tank capacity	82 liters (21.7 gallons)				

Model 250SE (1965-1968)

The 250SE model, introduced first at the Frankfurt Auto Show, was the fuel injected version of the 250S model. Both cars appeared identical. They shared the same body and running gear. The suspension system had been improved and the reinforced rear axle was equipped with the new hydro-pneumatic compensating spring. Larger wheels (14") and disc brakes all around were fitted.

The engine had a six-plunger fuel injection pump, with the fuel being injected intermittently into the suction pipe. Power output was rated at 150 horsepower at 5,500 revolutions per minute or 170 horsepower (SAE) at 5,600 revolutions per minute. As in the carburetor engine, maximum engine speed allowed was 6,300 revolutions per minute and the top speed of the 250SE sedan was 193 kilometers (120 miles) per hour.

In addition to the sedan, the elegant coupe and convertible were also available with the fuel-injection engine. The 220SE coupe and convertible — with identical bodies — were still being manufactured, but the more powerful version of the 250SE had, of course, better acceleration and higher maximum and cruising speed.

Prices

The 250SE four-door sedan sold for	DM 16,850
from April 1966 for	DM 17,350
The two-door coupe sold for	DM 24,350
from April 1966 for	DM 24,950
The two-door convertible sold for	DM 26,350
from April 1966 for	DM 26,950
Power steering	DM 550
Automatic transmission	DM 1,400

In the United States the sedan sold for in 1965

(East coast)	$ 6,331
(West coast)	$ 6,445
in September 1966 (East coast)	$ 6,385
in September 1967 (East coast)	$ 6,222
The 250SE coupe sold for in 1965 (East coast)	$ 8,890
in September 1966 (East coast)	$ 9,099
in September 1967 (East coast)	$ 9,099
The 250SE convertible sold for in 1965 (East coast)	$ 9,673
in September 1966 (East coast)	$ 9,892
in September 1967 (East coast)	$ 9,892
Power steering (1965)	$ 171
Automatic transmission	$ 342

Production

Production of the 250SE model [108 III] (from August/September 1965 until January 1968)

was in	1965	1,334 units
	1966	26,555 units
	1967	27,242 units
	1968	50 units
	total	55,181 units

Production of the 250SE coupe and convertible model [111 III] (from August/September 1965 until December 1967)

was in	1965	1,205 units
	1966	3,601 units
	1967	1,407 units
	total	6,213 units

Specifications

	250SE / 250SE (coupe and convertible)		
Engine type	6 cyl overhead camshaft (M 129)		
Bore and stroke	82 x 78.8mm (3.23 x 3.1 in)		
Displacement	2496 cc (152.3 cu in)		
Power output	150 hp (DIN) @ 5500 rpm (170 hp SAE @ 5600 rpm)		
Compression ratio	9.3:1		
Torque	22 mkg @ 4200 rpm (24 mkg SAE @ 4500 rpm 173.6 ft/lb)		
Fuel injection	Bosch six plunger pump		
Engine speed at 100 km/hr	3245 rpm		
Gear ratios	I. 4.05:1 automatic I. 3.98:1 (15.6) II. 2.23:1 II. 2.52:1 (9.88) III. 1.42:1 III. 1.58:1 (6.19) IV. 1.00:1 IV. 1.00:1 (3.92)		
Rear axle ratio	3.92		
Chassis	unit frame and body		
Suspension	independent front and rear, with coil springs, single joint swing axle		
Brakes and area	disc, servo assist, two circuit hydraulic, 273/279mm (10.75/10.99 in)		
Wheelbase	2750mm (108.3 in)		
Track, front/rear	1482/1485mm (58.3/58.5 in)		
Length	4900mm (192.9 in)	coupe: 4880mm (192.1 in)	conv: 4880mm (192.1 in)
Width	1810mm (71.3 in)	coupe: 1845mm (72.6 in)	conv: 1845mm (72.6 in)
Height	1440mm (56.7 in)	coupe: 1420mm (55.9 in)	conv: 1435mm (56.5 in)
Ground clearance	152mm (5.9 in)		
Tires	7.35 H 14 or 185 H 14	7.75 H 14 or 195 H 14	
Turning circle	12.1-11.9 meters (39 ft)		
Steering type and ratio	recirculating ball, 22.7:1 (4.1 turns); servo assisted 17.3:1 (3.2 turns)		
Weight	1510 kg (3322 lbs)	coupe: 1490 kg (3278 lbs)	conv: 1575 kg (3465 lbs)
Maximum speed	193 km/hr (120 mph); automatic: 188 km/hr (117 mph)		
Acceleration	12 sec 0-100 km/hr; automatic 13 sec 0-100 km/hr		
Fuel consumption	16 liters, super/100 km (14.7 mpg); automatic: 17 liters, super (13.7 mpg)		
Fuel tank capacity	82 liters (21.7 gallons)		

Prices

The 300SE four-door sedan sold for . . . . .DM 21,500
   from April 1966 for. . . . . .DM 22,100
The 300SEL four-door sedan sold for . . . . .DM 28,000
   from April 1966 for. . . . . .DM 28,600
The 300SE two-door coupe sold for . . . . .DM 31,350
   from April 1966 for. . . . . .DM 31,950
The 300SE two-door convertible sold for. . . . . .DM 33,350
   from April 1966 for. . . . . .DM 35,350
   Automatic transmission .DM 1,400
In the U.S. the price of the 300SE sedan was in 1965
   (East coast) . . . .$ 7,980
   (West coast) . . . .$ 9,980
   in September 1966 (East coast) . . . .$ 8,283
The price for the 300SEL sedan was in 1965
   (East coast) . . . .$ 9,863
   (West coast) . . . .$ 9,980
   in September 1966 (East coast) . . . .$ 10,144
The price for the 300SE coupe was in 1965
   (East coast) . . . .$ 11,511
   (West coast) . . . .$ 11,657
   in September 1966 (East coast) . . . .$ 11,807
The price for the 300SE convertible was in 1965
   (East coast) . . . .$ 12,295
   (West coast) . . . .$ 12,440
   in September 1966 (East coast) . . . .$ 12,591
   Power steering (1965) . . . .$ 171
   Automatic transmission (but standard equipment on the
     coupe and convertible models sold in the U.S.) . . .$ 342

Model 300SE (1965-1967)

The new 300SE, as well as the 300SEL, were also introduced to the public at the Frankfurt Auto Show in 1965. Both had the newly styled body. The longer car had a wheelbase of 2,850 millimeters (112.2 inches) just 100 millimeters (3.9 inches) longer than the regular sedan.

The six-cylinder light alloy fuel injection engine was equipped with the six-plunger pump which adjusted automatically to accelerator pedal pressure, engine speed, atmospheric pressure, and cooling water temperature, thus giving the best possible mixture for all driving conditions. Maximum power output was 170 horsepower at 5,400 revolutions per minute, or 190 horsepower (SAE) at 5,500 revolutions. With the regular 3.92 rear axle ratio and automatic transmission the car was capable of a maximum speed of 185 kilometers (115 miles) per hour. The faster ratio of 3.69 to 1 gave it 200 kilometer (124 miles) top speed (with manual transmission).

The elegant coupe and convertible models were also fitted with the 300SE engine and power train. These models had, however, the air suspension system, as did the 300SEL now.

Production

Production of the 300SE sedan [108 IV] (from August 1965 until December 1967)

was in	1965	214 units
	1966	1,989 units
	1967	534 units
	total	2,737 units

Production of the 300SEL sedan [109 III] (from September 1965/ March 1966 until December 1967)

was in	1965	1 unit
	1966	1,404 units
	1967	964 units
	total	2,369 units

Specifications

300SE / 300SEL / 300SE (coupe and convertible)

Engine type	6 cyl overhead camshaft (M 189)		
Bore and stroke	85 x 88mm (3.34 x 3.47 in)		
Displacement	2996 cc (182.8 cu in)		
Power output	170 hp (DIN) @ 5400 rpm (195 hp SAE @ 5500 rpm)		
Compression ratio	8.8:1		
Torque	25.4 mkg @ 4000 rpm (28.1 mkg @ 4100 rpm 203.3 ft/lb)		
Fuel injection	Bosch six plunger pump		
Engine speed at 100 km/hr	3245 rpm		

Gear ratios
		automatic	
I.	4.05:1	I.	3.98:1 (16.3)
II.	2.23:1	II.	2.52:1 (10.3)
III.	1.42:1	III.	1.58:1 (6.47)
IV.	1.00:1	IV.	1.00:1 (4.10)

Rear axle ratio	3.92 or 3.69		
Chassis	unit frame and body		
Suspension	independent front and rear, with coil springs, single joint swing axle		
Brakes and area	disc, servo assist, two circuit hydraulic, 273/279mm (10.75/10.99 in)		
Wheelbase	2750mm (108.3 in)	SEL: 2850mm (112.2 in)	
Track, front/rear	1482/1485mm (58.3/58.6 in)	SEL: rear 1490mm (58.7 in)	
Length	4900mm (192.9 in)	SEL: 5000mm (169.9 in)	coupe & conv: 4880mm (192in)
Width	1810mm (71.3 in)		coupe & conv: 1845mm (72.6 in)
Height	1440mm (56.7 in)	SEL: 1415mm (55.7 in)	coupe: 1395mm (54.9 in) conv: 1400mm (55.1 in)
Ground clearance	152mm (5.9 in)		
Tires	7.35 H 14 or 185 H 14		conv: 7.75 H 14 or 195 H 14
Turning circle	12.1-11.9 meters (39 ft)	SEL: 12.4-12.2 meters (40 ft)	coupe & conv: 12.1-11.9 meters (39 ft)
Steering type and ratio	recirculating ball, 17.3:1 (3.2 turns) servo assisted		
Weight	1575 kg (3465 lbs)	SEL: 1655 kg (3641 lbs)	coupe: 1650 kg (3630 lbs) conv: 1715 kg (3773 lbs)
Maximum speed	manual, 3.92 axle 190 km/hr (118 mph) automatic, 3.92 axle 185 km/hr (115 mph) manual, 3.69 axle 200 km/hr (124 mph) automatic, 369 axle 195 km/hr (121 mph)		
Acceleration	12 sec 0-100 km/hr		
Fuel consumption	17-19 liters, super/100 km (13.7 to 12.3 mpg)		
Fuel tank capacity	82 liters (21.7 gallons)		

Model 300SEL 6.3 (1968-1972)

The 300SEL 6.3 model was introduced in the United States in June 1968, quite appropriately at the Laguna Seca race course, with Rudolf Uhlenhaut in attendance. He pointed out that the car had better road-holding ability, braking potential, suspension stability, and maneuverability than any comparable automobile in the world. It had first been shown in Europe in March 1968.

With the 6,332 cubic centimeter fuel-injected 300-horsepower (SAE) V-8 engine installed in the slightly modified but outwardly regular sedan body of the New Generation type, the car weighed 3,835 pounds and had a power-to-weight ratio of 12.8 pounds per horsepower. Performance was truly fantastic, especially when Uhlenhaut demonstrated to us the car's abilities. Zero to 60 miles acceleration took 6.5 seconds and the maximum speed of the 6.3 was 137 miles (220 kilometers) per hour.

The sedan had the air suspension system of the 600 series and many extra features were included as standard items, such as air conditioning, radio, leather upholstery, power steering, and power windows. Except for the numbers 6.3 on the trunk lid, the car was not distinguishable from the regular 300SEL model.

After exhaustively testing the car, *Road & Track* magazine called it "the greatest sedan in the world" and summarized the test, stating that the 6.3 was "truly the executive road racer . . . does more different things well than any other single car." This author concurred. The 300SEL 6.3 was certainly an outstanding automobile in every way.

Prices and Production

The 300SEL 6.3 four-door sedan sold in 1968 for . . . . .DM	39,160
in 1969 . . . . .DM	39,500
in 1970 . . . . .DM	43,180
in 1971 . . . . .DM	45,400
The 300SEL 6.3 sedan sold in the U.S. (when introduced) for . . . .$	13,998
The price was in September 1968 (East coast). . . . .$	14,065
in October 1969 (East coast) . . . .$	14,530
in October 1970 (East coast) . . . .$	15,875
in March 1971 (East coast) . . . .$	16,275

Production of the 300SEL 6.3 sedan [109 E63] (from December 1967 until September 1972)

was in	1967	1 unit
	1968	1,094 units
	1969	2,578 units
	1970	1,797 units
	1971	670 units
	1972	386 units
	total	6,526 units

Specifications

	300SEL 6.3
Engine type	V-8 cyl overhead camshaft for each cylinder bank (M 100)
Bore and stroke	103 x 95mm (4.06 x 3.74 in)
Displacement	6332 cc (386.3 cu in)
Power output	250 hp (DIN) @ 4000 rpm (300 hp SAE @ 4100 rpm)
Compression ratio	9.0:1
Torque	51 mkg @ 2800 rpm 369 ft/lb (60 mkg SAE @ 3000 rpm 434 ft/lb)
Fuel injection	Bosch eight plunger pump
Engine speed at 100 km/hr	2510 rpm
Gear ratios	I. 3.98:1 (11.34) II. 2.46:1 (7.00) III. 1.58:1 (4.50) IV. 1.00:1 (2.85)
Rear axle ratio	2.85
Chassis	unit frame and body
Suspension	independent front and rear, air springs, self leveling and air suspension, single joint swing axle
Brakes and area	disc, ventilated, servo assist, two circuit hydraulic, 273/279mm (107.5/109.9 in)
Wheelbase	2850mm (112.2 in)
Track, front/rear	1482/1490mm (58.3/58.7 in)
Length	5000mm (196.9 in)
Width	1810mm (71.3 in)
Height	1410mm (55.5 in)
Ground clearance	160mm (6.3 in)
Tires	FR 70 VR 14 (Dunlop) 205 VR 14 L
Turning circle	12.2 meters (40.4 ft)
Steering type and ratio	recirculating ball, 15.7:1 (3.0 turns)
Weight	1740 kg (3828 lbs)
Maximum speed	220 km/hr (137 mph)
Acceleration	6.5 sec 0-100 km/hr
Fuel consumption	15.5 liters, super/100 km (15.2 mpg)
Fuel tank capacity	105 liters (27.7 gallons)

Prices and Production

The 200 four-door sedan sold in 1968 for . . . . .DM 11,500
    in 1970 for. . . . . .DM 12,745
    in 1972 for. . . . . .DM 13,390
    in 1974 for. . . . . .DM 15,140
    in 1975 for. . . . . .DM 16,710
    Power steering . . . . .DM   515
    Automatic transmission . . . . .DM 1,440
The 200 sedan sold in the U.S. first for (East coast). . . .$ 4,360
    in September 1968 (East coast) for. . . . .$ 4,450
    in October 1969 (East coast) for . . . .$ 4,680
    in October 1970 (East coast) for . . . .$ 5,217
    Power steering (1970) . . . .$ 198
    Automatic transmission . . . .$ 392

Production of the 200 model [115 V20] (from October 1967/
January 1968)

	was in	1967	67 units
		1968	20,954 units
		1969	26,138 units
		1970	29,733 units
		1971	35,122 units
		1972	40,562 units
		1973	37,337 units
		1974	37,640 units
		1975	48,214 units
		total	275,767 units

Model 200 (1967-   )

The new 200 sedan was the least expensive car of the fifteen models of the New Generation class, introduced to the public in January 1968. All of the four- and smaller six-cylinder models shared the same body and basic construction. At the Frankfurt Auto Show in 1967 the main emphasis was placed on safety rather than on speed. Such safety features as collapsible steering column, padded instrument panel with softer knobs and soft ignition key, breakaway rear mirror, and seatback locks activated by the doors were standard equipment. The body was designed for maximum crash resistance and the front and rear ends for easier crushing in collisions to protect the passengers in the vehicle. A new rear axle was designed for improved roadability. Fourteen-inch wheels were again used on these new models and they had a slightly longer (50 mm = 2 inch) wheelbase and a narrower track. The entire instrument panel was also redesigned for improved legibility.

The engine for the 200 model was of the proven type and only minor improvements were made in it. The 1,988 cubic centimeter four-cylinder powerplant developed 95 DIN horsepower and 122.2 ft/lbs. torque, as it had in the former model. All performance figures were identical.

In 1972 all of the smaller models were equipped with the new, safer four-spoke steering wheel. In 1973, because of the fuel crisis, the compression of the engine was lowered to 8 to 1, so that normal octane gasoline could be used. That engine developed 85 DIN horsepower instead of the former 95.

Specifications

	200
Engine type	4 cyl overhead camshaft (M 115)
Bore and stroke	87 x 83.6mm (3.43 x 3.29 in)
Displacement	1988 cc (121.27 cu in)
Power output	95 hp (DIN) @ 5200 rpm (105 hp SAE @ 5400 rpm)
Compression ratio	9.0:1
Torque	15.7 mkg @ 3600 rpm (16.9 mkg @ 3800 rpm 122.2 ft/lb)
Carburetion	2 downdraft carburetors Solex 38 PCSJ
Engine speed at 100 km/hr	3310 rpm

Gear ratios			automatic	
I.	4.09:1	3.90:1	I.	3.98:1
II.	2.25:1	2.30:1	II.	2.52:1
III.	1.42:1	1.41:1	III.	1.58:1
IV.	1.00:1	1.00:1	IV.	1.00:1

Rear axle ratio	3.92 (4.08 for U.S.)
Chassis	unit frame and body
Suspension	independent front and rear, with coil springs, diagonal-pivot swing axle, anti-sway bars
Brakes and area	disc, power assisted standard, 273/279mm (10.75/10.99 in)
Wheelbase	2750mm (108.3 in)
Track, front/rear	1440/1434mm (56.7/56.5 in)
Length	4680mm (184.3 in)
Width	1770mm (69.7 in)
Height	1440mm (56.7 in)
Ground clearance	175mm (6.9 in)
Tires	6.95 x 14 or 175 x 14
Turning circle	11.7 meters (38.4 ft)
Steering type and ratio	recirculating ball (4.6 turns); servo assisted (4.0 turns)
Weight	1275 kg (2805 lbs)
Maximum speed	161 km/hr (100 mph); automatic: 158 km/hr (98 mph)
Acceleration	15 sec 0-100 km/hr; automatic: 16 sec 0-100 km/hr
Fuel consumption	12.5 liters, super/100 km (18.75 mpg); automatic: 13.5 liters, super (17.4 mpg)
Fuel tank capacity	65 liters (17.2 gallons)

Model 200D (1967-   )

The 200D model was, as previously, the same as the gasoline-engined sedan of that size. One of the fifteen New Generation models, it shared the body style along with all of the new safety features and construction changes made for the 1968 model year. The body was nearly the same as that of the 250S line of 1966, which had a lower silhouette, lower center of gravity, and wider radiator design in the traditional manner, of course.

The engine of the 200D was the same as that of the earlier model. Displacing 1,988 cubic centimeters and developing 55 DIN (60 SAE) horsepower and 87 ft/lb. torque, it gave this economical diesel-engined model a most satisfactory performance. Power steering and power brakes were optional items, as was automatic transmission.

As before, the diesel version of the smaller model marketed by Daimler-Benz was again a best-seller and more of these 200D sedans were sold than those of the gasoline-powered version. The diesel cars offered actually the same comforts as the others and had in addition the tremendous cost advantages inherent only not in the simpler maintenance of the diesel engine, but also the economy of fuel, both in lower initial cost and in increased mileage achieved.

Prices and Production

The 200D four-door sedan sold in 1968 for . . . . .DM 12,000
in 1970 for. . . . . .DM 13,265
in 1972 for. . . . . .DM 14,430
in 1974 for. . . . . .DM 15,585
in 1975 for. . . . . .DM 17,185
Power steering . . . . .DM   515
Automatic transmission . . . . .DM 1,440
The 200D sedan sold in the U.S. first for (East coast). . .$ 4,494
in September 1968 (East coast) for. . . . .$ 4,580
in October 1969 (East coast) for . . . .$ 4,782
in Ocotber 1970 (East coast) for . . . .$ 5,324
Power steering (1970) . . . .$ 198
Automatic transmission . . . .$ 392

Production of the 200D model [115 D20] (from October 1967/
January 1968)

was in 1967	106 units	
1968	23,293 units	
1969	27,663 units	
1970	32,841 units	
1971	35,000 units	
1972	41,065 units	
1973	45,287 units	
1974	50,613 units	
1975	62,978 units	
total	318,846 units	

Specifications

	200D
Engine type	4 cyl diesel, overhead camshaft (OM 615)
Bore and stroke	87 x 83.6mm (3.43 x 3.29 in)
Displacement	1988 cc (121.27 cu in)
Power output	55 hp (DIN) @ 4200 rpm (61 hp SAE @ 4200 rpm)
Compression ratio	21:1
Torque	11.5 mkg @ 2400 rpm (83.2 ft/lb)
Fuel injection	Bosch four plunger pump
Engine speed at 100 km/hr	3375 rpm
Gear ratios	I. 3.90:1 II. 2.30:1 III. 1.41:1 IV. 1.00:1
Rear axle ratio	3.92 (for U.S. 4.08)
Chassis	unit frame and body
Suspension	independent front and rear, with coil springs, diagonal-pivot swing axle, anti-sway bars
Brakes and area	disc, power assisted standard, 273/279mm (10.75/10.99 in)
Wheelbase	2750mm (108.3 in)
Track, front/rear	1440/1434mm (56.7/56.5 in)
Length	4680mm (184.3 in)
Width	1770mm (69.7 in)
Height	1440mm (56.7 in)
Ground clearance	175mm (6.9 in)
Tires	6.95 x 14 or 175 x 14
Turning circle	11.7 meters (38.4 ft)
Steering type and ratio	recirculating ball, (4.6 turns), servo assisted (4.0 turns)
Weight	1350 kg (2970 lbs)
Maximum speed	130 km/hr (81 mph)
Acceleration	30 sec 0-100 km/hr
Fuel consumption	8.1 liters/100 km (29 mpg)
Fuel tank capacity	65 liters (17.2 gallons)

Model 220 (1967-1973)

The 220 model was basically the same car as the smaller-engined one. It was the third of the New Generation models to share the same body style, including all of the new safety features. It was meant to replace the 200 sedan in the United States market.

Over the previous model, this new style featured the lower silhouette, an increased wheelbase and narrower track, offered increased visibility, a new headlight treatment with the lower half of the unit having amber color, and protective strips with rubber inserts all around the body. The single front and rear bumpers also had a rubber insert for added scratch protection. New larger rear light clusters had been designed for brighter, improved visibility.

The engine had two single throat Solex carburetors and developed 116 SAE horsepower at 5,200 revolutions per minute and torque of 142 ft/lbs. at 3,000 revolutions. Maximum speed was 100 miles per hour.

Optional equipment was the power assisted steering, air conditioning, sliding sun roof, leather upholstery, power windows, and other features. The base price of the 220 sedan was $4,360 on the East coast in 1968.

Prices and Production

The 220 four-door sedan sold in 1968 for . . . . .DM 12,000
   in 1970 for. . . . . .DM 13,165
   in 1972 for. . . . . .DM 14,375
   in 1973 for. . . . . .DM 14,985
   Power steering . . . . .DM   515
   Automatic transmission .DM 1,440
The 220 sedan sold in the United States in January 1968 for
   (East coast) . . . .$ 4,360
   (West coast) . . . .$ 4,446
   in September 1971, including automatic transmission
     (East coast) . . . .$ 6,206
   in September 1972, including automatic transmission
     (East coast) . . . .$ 6,560
   in March 1973, including automatic transmission
     (East coast) . . . .$ 6,889
   Power steering (1970) . . . .$ 198
   Power steering (1973) . . . .$ 251
   Automatic transmission (1970) . . . .$ 392

Production of the 220 model [115 V22] (from October 1967/
February 1968 until August 1973)

was in	1967	131 units
	1968	23,486 units
	1969	22,493 units
	1970	22,652 units
	1971	24,140 units
	1972	23,691 units
	1973	12,146 units
	total	128,739 units

Specifications

	220
Engine type	4 cyl overhead camshaft (M 115)
Bore and stroke	87.0 x 92.4mm (3.43 x 3.64 in)
Displacement	2197 cc (134 cu in)
Power output	105 hp (DIN) (116 hp SAE) @ 5200 rpm
Compression ratio	9:1
Torque	17.5 mkg @ 3600 rpm (19.7 mkg @ 3000 rpm 142.5 ft/lb)
Carburetion	2 dual downdraft carburetors Solex 36/40 PDSI (U.S.: 2 Stromberg carburetors 175 CDT)
Engine speed at 100 km/hr	3300 rpm
Gear ratios	I. 3.90:1 II. 2.30:1 III. 1.41:1 IV. 1.00:1
Rear axle ratio	3.92 (4.08 for U.S.)
Chassis	unit frame and body
Suspension	independent front and rear, with coil springs, diagonal pivot swing axle, anti-sway bars
Brakes and area	disc, power assist standard, 273/279mm (10.75/10.99 in)
Wheelbase	2750mm (108.3 in)
Track, front/rear	1440/1434mm (56.7/56.5 in)
Length	4680mm (184.3 in)
Width	1770mm (69.7 in)
Height	1440mm (56.7 in)
Ground clearance	175mm (6.9 in)
Tires	6.95 x 14 or 175 x 14
Turning circle	11.7 meters (38.4 ft)
Steering type and ratio	recirculating ball (4.6 turns); servo assisted (4.0 turns)
Weight	1314 kg (2890 lbs)
Maximum speed	161 km/hr (100 mph)
Acceleration	14 sec 0-100 km/hr
Fuel consumption	12 liters, super/100 km (19.5 mpg)
Fuel tank capacity	65 liters (17.2 gallons)

Prices and Production

The 220D four-door sedan sold in 1968 for . . . . .DM 12,500
    in 1970 for. . . . . .DM 13,690
    in 1972 for. . . . . .DM 14,930
    in 1973 for. . . . . .DM 15,485
Power steering . . . . .DM   515
Automatic transmission .DM 1,440
The 220D long limousine sold in 1969 for . . . . .DM 18,315
    the price rose yearly until 1975 it was . . . . .DM 26,075
The 220D sedan sold in the U.S. in January 1968 for
    (East coast) . . . .$ 4,494
    (West coast) . . . .$ 4,580
    in September 1971 (East coast) . . . .$ 5,900
    in September 1972 (East coast) . . . .$ 6,345
    in March 1973 (East coast) . . . .$ 6,662
        with automatic transmission . . . .$ 7,100
    Power steering (1970) . . . .$ 198
    Power steering (1973) . . . .$ 251
    Automatic transmission (1970) . . . .$ 392

Production of the 220D model [115 D22] (from July 1967/
January 1968)

was in	1967	364 units
	1968	50,630 units
	1969	59,628 units
	1970	63,314 units
	1971	64,297 units
	1972	73,729 units
	1973	54,321 units
	1974	27,510 units
	1975	21,226 units
	total	415,019 units

Model 220D (1967-   )

The 220D was the fourth of the New Generation cars to share the same body style with the 200-220-200D models. It, too, was introduced to replace the smaller sedan in the United States market.

All of the outward specifications were identical with the gasoline version of this model. It was the luxury edition of the economical and reliable diesel-powerd automobile which actually went back to 1936 when a diesel passenger car was first built by Mercedes-Benz.

The four-speed manual transmission was standard, either column or floor mounted. Automatic transmission was an optional extra, as were power brakes and power steering.

The 2.2-liter diesel engine had Bosch four-plunger fuel injection and a five main bearing crankshaft. With the usual 21:1 compression ratio and maximum torque of 96 ft/lbs. at 2,400 revolutions per minute, the engine developed 65 SAE horsepower at 4,200 revolutions per minute and gave the car a maximum and cruising speed of over 80 miles per hour. (This diesel engine met the U.S. government standards for emission of hydrocarbons, carbon monoxide, and oxide of nitrogens through 1974, and the CO limit for 1975.)

Symbolic of the popularity of the diesel automobile, on May 9, 1968, the two millionth passenger car to come off the assembly lines at the Sindelfingen plant since 1946 was a 220D model — cream-colored and flower-covered.

A long wheelbase model sedan became available in December 1968. It had seats for eight persons and was similar to the 230 long limousine. The wheelbase was 3,400 mm (133.86 in) weight was 1,540 kg (3,388 lbs). Maximum speed was 130 km/hr (81 mph) and fuel consumption 11 liters per 100 km. With the optional automatic transmission, these figures were 125 km/hr and 12 liters/100 km (18 miles per gallon).

Specifications

	220D
Engine type	4 cyl diesel, overhead camshaft (OM 615)
Bore and stroke	87.0 x 92.4mm (3.43 x 3.64 in)
Displacement	2197 cc (134 cu in)
Power output	60 hp (DIN) (65 hp SAE) @ 4200 rpm
Compression ratio	21:1
Torque	12.8 mkg @ 2400 rpm (92.6 ft/lb)
Fuel injection	Bosch four plunger pump
Engine speed at 100 km/hr	3375 rpm
Gear ratios	I. 3.90:1 (15.37) II. 2.30:1 (9.01) III. 1.41:1 (5.52) IV. 1.00:1 (3.92)
Rear axle ratio	3.92 (for U.S. 4.08)
Chassis	unit frame and body
Suspension	independent front and rear, with coil springs, diagonal-pivot swing axle, anti-sway bars
Brakes and area	disc, power assist standard, 273/279mm (10.75/10.99 in)
Wheelbase	2750mm (108.3 in)
Track, front/rear	1440/1434mm (56.7/56.5 in)
Length	4680mm (184.3 in)
Width	1770mm (69.7 in)
Height	1440mm (56.7 in)
Ground clearance	175mm (6.9 in)
Tires	6.95 x 14 or 175 x 14
Turning circle	11.7 meters (38.4 ft)
Steering type and ratio	recirculating ball, (4.6 turns); servo assisted 22.7:1 (4.0 turns)
Weight	1363 kg (2997 lbs)
Maximum speed	135 km/hr (84 mph)
Acceleration	28.1 sec 0-100 km/hr
Fuel consumption	8.5 liters/100 km (27.75 mpg)
Fuel tank capacity	65 liters (17.2 gallons)

Model 230 (1967-   )

The 230 model, in the center of the medium price range of the New Generation cars, had the same body style as that of the 200, 220, and the 250 sedans. It replaced the former 230 model, first built in 1965.

The interior dimensions were the same as those of the other models which shared the body style, the rear center arm rest, larger door pockets, increased visibility (11 percent more glass area), arm rests on all doors, and roof-mounted assist handles, but it had the grip handles attached to the arm rest of the right front door, while the 250 model had them on all three doors (except the driver's).

The engine of the 230 model was the same as before, except for redesigned cams which improved the torque at lower engine speeds and molybdenum coated piston rings (1, 2 and 3) for longer wear and reduced oil consumption. The new gear box and newly designed clutch, now with new diaphragm spring clutch having fewer moving parts (that is, one diaphram spring instead of nine pressure springs), were fitted to all of the models which had the same chassis and body as the 230 sedan. The new hydro-pneumatic leveling device, automatic transmission, and power steering were optional items.

A long-wheelbase sedan to seat eight passengers became available in October 1968. It was also made with the 220D engine two months later. The wheelbase was 3,400 mm (133.86 in) and the total weight was 1,515 kg (3,344 lbs). The maximum speed was 170 km/hr (106 mph) and fuel consumption 16 liters per 100 kilometers. With automatic transmission these figures were 165 km/hr and 17 liters/100 km.

Prices and Production

The 230 four-door sedan sold in 1968 for . . . . .DM 13,150
   in 1970 for. . . . . .DM 14,620
   in 1972 for. . . . . .DM 16,100
   in 1973 for. . . . . .DM 16,765
   Power steering . . . . .DM   515
   Automatic transmission . . . . .DM 1,440
The 230 long limousine sold in 1968 for . . . . .DM 18,980
   the price rose gradually every year and in 1975 was . .DM 26,685
The 230 four-door sedan sold in the United States
   in January 1968 for (East coast). . . . .$ 4,544
      (West coast) . . . .$ 4,631
   in December 1968 (East coast). . . . .$ 4,764
   Power steering (1970) . . . .$ 198
   Automatic transmission . . . .$ 392

Production of the 230 model [114 V23] (from September 1967/ January 1968)

	was in	1967	252 units
		1968	22,064 units
		1969	23,835 units
		1970	25,252 units
		1971	30,520 units
		1972	35,270 units
		1973	31,378 units
		1974	25,314 units
		1975	22,992 units
		total	216,877 units

Specifications

	230
Engine type	6 cyl overhead camshaft (M 180)
Bore and stroke	81.7 x 72.8mm (3.23 x 2.87 in)
Displacement	2292 cc (139.9 cu in)
Power output	120 hp (DIN) @ 5400 rpm (135 hp SAE @ 5600 rpm)
Compression ratio	9:1
Torque	18.2 mkg @ 3600 rpm; 20 mkg @ 3800 rpm (144.7 ft/lb)
Carburetion	2 dual downdraft carburetors Zenith 35/40 INAT
Engine speed at 100 km/hr	3180 rpm
Gear ratios	I. 3.90:1 II. 2.30:1 III. 1.41:1 IV. 1.00:1
Rear axle ratio	3.92 (4.08 for U.S.)
Chassis	unit frame and body
Suspension	independent front and rear, with coil springs, diagonal-pivot swing axle, anti-sway bars
Brakes and area	disc, power assist standard, 273/279mm (10.95/10.99 in)
Wheelbase	2750mm (108.3 in)
Track, front/rear	1444/1440mm (56.9/56.7 in)
Length	4680mm (184.3 in)
Width	1770mm (69.7 in)
Height	1440mm (56.7 in)
Ground clearance	175mm (6.9 in)
Tires	6.95 x 14 or 175 x 14
Turning circle	11.7 meters (38.4 ft)
Steering type and ratio	recirculating ball (4.6 turns); servo assisted (4.0 turns)
Weight	1323 kg (2911 lbs)
Maximum speed	165 km/hr (102 mph)
Acceleration	14 sec 0-100 km/hr
Fuel consumption	11.2 liters, super/100 km (21 mpg)
Fuel tank capacity	65 liters (17.2 gallons)

Model 250 (1967-1972)

The 250 model represented the top of the medium price range in the passenger car production line of the New Generation cars. It was distinguished by several styling refinements over the others which shared the body with this model. As the 230 model, it was fitted with a wider-spaced grill design — the box type instead of the pierced type which the 200 and 220 models had. The 250 also had a double bumper on the front and a chrome door strip.

The six-cylinder engine for the 250 was newly developed. It produced 146 SAE horsepower at 5,600 revolutions per minute. Suspension was the same as the other, less expensive models, which shared the same body style. The optional hydro-pneumatic leveler controlled the rear suspension unit, leveling the car when loaded. It had the advantage of constant leveling because the system was operative when the engine was running and maintained a constant bumper height.

Prices and Production

The 250 four-door sedan sold in 1967 for . . . . .DM 14,630
   in 1970 for. . . . . .DM 16,185
   in 1972 for. . . . . .DM 17,875
Power steering . . . . .DM   515
Automatic transmission . . . . .DM 1,440
The 250 four-door sedan sold in the United States
   in January 1968 for (East coast). . . . .$ 5,060
     (West coast) . . . .$ 5,150
   in October 1969 (East coast) . . . .$ 5,208
   in October 1970 (including automatic transmission)
    (East coast) . . . .$ 6,208
   in September 1971 (including automatic transmission)
    (East coast) . . . .$ 7,205
Power steering (1970) . . . .$ 198

Production of the 250 model [114 V25] (from July/December 1967 until May 1972)

was in	1967	2,215 units
	1968	20,475 units
	1969	18,692 units
	1970	17,329 units
	1971	15,180 units
	1972	4,412 units
	total	78,303 units

Specifications

	250
Engine type	6 cyl overhead camshaft (M 114)
Bore and stroke	81.7 x 78.8mm (3.23 x 3.1 in)
Displacement	2496 cc (152.4 cu in)
Power output	130 hp (DIN) @ 5000 rpm (146 hp SAE @ 5600 rpm)
Compression ratio	9:1
Torque	20 mkg @ 3600 rpm (22.2 mkg @ 3800 rpm 161 ft/lb)
Carburetion	2 dual downdraft carburetors Zenith 35/40 INAT
Engine speed at 100 km/hr	3180 rpm
Gear ratios	I. 3.90:1 II. 2.30:1 III. 1.41:1 IV. 1.00:1
Rear axle ratio	3.92 (4.08 for U.S.)
Chassis	unit frame and body
Suspension	independent front and rear, with coil springs, diagonal-pivot swing axle, anti-sway bars
Brakes and area	disc, power assist standard, 273/279mm (10.8/11.0 in)
Wheelbase	2750mm (108.3 in)
Track, front/rear	1444/1440mm (56.9/56.7 in)
Length	4680mm (184.3 in)
Width	1770mm (69.7 in)
Height	1440mm (56.7 in)
Ground clearance	175mm (6.9 in)
Tires	6.95 H 14 or 175 x 14
Turning circle	11.7 meters (38.4 ft)
Steering type and ratio	recirculating ball (4.6 turns); servo assisted (4.0 turns)
Weight	1370 kg (3014 lbs)
Maximum speed	180 km/hr (112 mph)
Acceleration	13 sec 0-100 km/hr
Fuel consumption	12.5 liters, super/100 km (18.75 mpg)
Fuel tank capacity	65 liters (17.2 gallons)

Prices and Production

The 280S four-door sedan sold in 1968 for. . . . . .DM 17,000
   in 1970 for. . . . . .DM 18,815
   in 1971 for. . . . . .DM 19,760
   Power steering . . . . .DM   515
   Automatic transmission . . . . .DM 1,440
The 280S four-door sedan sold in the United States
   in January 1968 for (East coast). . . . .$ 5,897
    (West coast) . . . .$ 6,011
   in October 1969 (East coast) . . . .$ 6,273
   in October 1970 (including automatic transmission)
    (East coast) . . . .$ 7,019
   in March 1971 (including automatic transmission)
    (East coast) . . . .$ 7,370
   Power steering (1970) . . . .$ 198

Production of the 280S model [108 V28] (from November 1967/
January 1968 until September 1972)

was in	1967	762 units
	1968	20,110 units
	1969	25,249 units
	1970	24,882 units
	1971	16,234 units
	1972	6,429 units
	total	93,666 units

Model 280S (1967-1972)

The 280S model was the lowest priced car in the higher priced range of the New Generation automobiles. The body style was that of the new 280SE and the 300SE models, as well as that of the older 250S first introduced in 1965 which remained in production.

The body was longer than that of the smaller-engined cars by 8.4 inches, but the wheelbase remained at 108.3 inches. Track was slightly larger and these sedans were somewhat wider, allowing more inside room for the passengers. A longer version, the SEL, was also available, with a wheelbase of 112.2 inches but otherwise the same specifications as the regular sedan. A distinctive difference was the arrangement of the head lights. Two vertical lights made up the cluster which in the other models consisted of one headlight and amber indicator and parking lights.

The engine had the dual downdraft carburetor, air oil cooler, and a new cylinder arrangement for increased cooling, and developed 140 (DIN) horsepower at 5,200 (or 157 SAE at 5,400) revolutions per minute. The seven-bearing crankshaft made for quieter and more flexible operation of this newly designed powerplant.

Specifications

	280S
Engine type	6 cyl overhead camshaft (M 130)
Bore and stroke	86.5 x 78.8mm (3.41 x 3.10 in)
Displacement	2778 cc (169.5 cu in)
Power output	140 hp (DIN) @ 5200 rpm (157 hp SAE @ 5400 rpm)
Compression ratio	9:1
Torque	23 mkg @ 3600 rpm (25.1 mkg @ 3800 rpm 181.6 ft/lb)
Carburetion	2 dual downdraft carburetors Zenith 35/40 INAT
Engine speed at 100 km/hr	3140 rpm
Gear ratios	I. 3.90:1 II. 2.30:1 III. 1.41:1 IV. 1.00:1
Rear axle ratio	3.92 (4.08 for U.S.)
Chassis	unit frame and body
Suspension	independent front and rear, with coil springs, diagonal-pivot swing axle, anti-sway bars
Brakes and area	disc, power assist standard, 273/279mm (10.8/11.0 in)
Wheelbase	2750mm (108.3 in)
Track, front/rear	1444/1440mm (56.9/56.7 in)
Length	4680mm (184.3 in)
Width	1770mm (69.7 in)
Height	1440mm (56.7 in)
Ground clearance	175mm (6.9 in)
Tires	7.35 H 14
Turning circle	12.5 meters (41 ft)
Steering type and ratio	recirculating ball (4.0 turns); servo assisted (3.0 turns)
Weight	1460 kg (3212 lbs)
Maximum speed	185 km/hr (115 mph); automatic: 180 km/hr (112 mph)
Acceleration	12.5 sec 0-100 km/hr
Fuel consumption	12.5 liters/100 km (18.75 mpg)
Fuel tank capacity	82 liters (21.7 gallons)

Production

Production of the 280SE model [108 E28] (from November 1967/
January 1968 until September 1972)

was in	1967	365 units
	1968	18,685 units
	1969	25,081 units
	1970	25,627 units
	1971	14,871 units
	1972	6,422 units
	total	91,051 units

Production of the 280SEL model [108 E28] (from January 1968
until April 1971)

was in	1968	1,688 units
	1969	2,610 units
	1970	3,674 units
	1971	278 units
	total	8,250 units

Production of the 280SE coupe and convertible model [111 E28]
(from November 1967/February 1968 until May 1971)

was in	1968	55 units
	1969	1,950 units
	1970	2,501 units
	1971	613 units
	1972	68 units
	total	5,187 units

Model 280SE (1967-1972)

The 280SE model was available as a sedan and the more luxurious coupe and convertible. The sedan body was the same as that of the 280S New Generation model, but the coupe and convertible had the same body style as the earlier 250SE which they replaced, and which were discontinued. There were no distinguishing marks between these two 280 line sedans, except, of course, for the engine. The interior was no more elegant than that of the carburetor-engined car but the overall weight of the SE was fifty pounds more.

The fuel injected six-cylinder engine had a six-plunger pump for increased engine performance with improved economy and was not affected by altitude or by temperature. It also provided an efficient smog control system. Otherwise the 2.8-liter engines were alike. The seven main bearing crankshaft made for less vibration and longer bearing life and the greater separation between cylinders ensured better cooling. The new viscose cooling fan was also more efficient and the redesigned cams and molybdenum covered rings were all appreciable improvements. The 280SE engine developed 160 (DIN) horsepower at 5,500 (or 180 SAE at 5,750) revolutions per minute.

The 280SEL sedan went into production in January 1968. It had a longer wheelbase, by 3.9 inches, than the regular sedan, but otherwise was the same car in practically every respect.

Prices

The 280SE four-door sedan sold in 1968 for	.DM 18,600
in 1970 for	.DM 20,535
in 1971 for	.DM 21,590
The 280SEL four-door sedan sold in 1968 for	.DM 25,100
The 280SE coupe sold in 1968 for	.DM 26,510
in 1970 for	.DM 29,140
in 1971 for	.DM 30,680
The 280SE convertible sold in 1968 for	.DM 28,510
in 1970 for	.DM 31,140
in 1971 for	.DM 32,680
Power steering	.DM 515
Automatic transmission	.DM 1,440
The 280SE four-door sedan sold in the United States	
in January 1968 for (East coast)	$ 6,222
(West coast)	$ 6,336
in October 1969 (East coast)	$ 6,561
in September 1968 (East coast)	$ 6,310
in October 1970 (including automatic transmission)	
(East coast)	$ 7,297
in September 1971 (including automatic transmission)	
(East coast)	$ 9,546
The 280SEL sedan sold in January 1968 for	
(East coast)	$ 6,622
(West coast)	$ 6,712
in September 1968 (East coast)	$ 6,722
in October 1969 (East coast)	$ 6,992
in October 1970 (including automatic transmission)	
(East coast)	$ 8,088
in September 1971 (including automatic transmission)	
(East coast)	$ 10,925
The 280SE coupe sold in January 1968 for (East coast)	$ 9,174
(West coast)	$ 9,262
in September 1968 (East coast)	$ 9,424
in October 1969 (East coast)	$ 11,112
in January 1970 (East coast)	$ 11,612
The 280SE convertible sold in January 1968 for	
(East coast)	$ 9,967
(West coast)	$ 10,054
in September 1968 (East coast)	$ 10,217
in October 1969 (East coast)	$ 11,924
in January 1970 (East coast)	$ 12,444
Power steering (1970) (standard on SEL model)	$ 198
Automatic transmission	$ 392

Specifications

280SE / 280SEL / 280SE (coupe and convertible)	
Engine type	6 cyl overhead camshaft (M 130)
Bore and stroke	86.5 x 78.8mm (3.41 x 3.10 in)
Displacement	2778 cc (169.5 cu in)
Power output	160 hp (DIN) @ 5500 rpm (180 hp SAE @ 5750 rpm)
Compression ratio	9.5:1
Torque	24.5 mkg @ 4250 rpm (26.7 mkg @ 4500 rpm 193.2 ft/lb)
Fuel injection	Bosch six plunger pump
Engine speed at 100 km/hr	3140 rpm
Gear ratios	I. 3.98:1 II. 2.39:1 III. 1.46:1 IV. 1.00:1
Rear axle ratio	3.92 (4.08 for U.S.)
Chassis	unit frame and body
Suspension	independent front and rear, with coil springs, diagonal-pivot swing axle, anti-sway bars
Brakes and area	disc, power assisted, standard, 273/279mm (10.8/11.0 in)
Wheelbase	2750mm (108.3 in) SEL: 2850mm (112.2 in)
Track, front/rear	1482/1490mm (58.4/58.7 in)
Length	4680mm (184.3 in) SEL: 4780mm (188.2 in)
Width	1770mm (69.7 in) coupe and conv: 72.6 in
Height	1440mm (56.7 in) coupe: 55.9 in; conv: 56.5 in
Ground clearance	175mm (6.9 in)
Tires	7.35 H 14 or 185 H 14
Turning circle	12.5 meters (41 ft) SEL: (42 ft)
Steering type and ratio	recirculating ball (4.0 turns); servo assisted (3.0 turns)
Weight	1486 kg (3270 lbs) SEL: 3305 lbs coupe: 3330 lbs conv: 3495 lbs
Maximum speed	190 km/hr (118 mph); automatic: 185 km/hr (115 mph)
Acceleration	10.5 sec 0-100 km/hr
Fuel consumption	12.5 liters, super/100 km (18.75 mpg)
Fuel tank capacity	82 liters (21.7 gallons)

Model 300SEL (1967-1970)

The 300SEL sedan was the top of the line of New Generation cars for 1968. It retained the body of the former 300SE, first built in 1965, but now came equipped with the fuel injection engine of 2,778 cubic centimeter displacement and 180 SAE horsepower. The only outward difference between this and the 280 line was a more generous use of chrome around the window areas. Inwardly, the furnishings were of the finest as befitting this most elegant limousine of the New Generation class. Only the great 600 automobiles were more luxuriously built.

Such optional extras as automatic transmission, power steering, and air suspension system were standard on the 300SEL sedan. The body dimensions and chassis specifications were practically the same as those for the 300SEL 6.3 model, and the price of the car surely indicated that it was a superb automobile.

Prices and Production

The 300SEL four-door sedan sold in 1968 for . . . . . . .DM 29,760
The 300SEL sedan sold in the United States
    in January 1968 for (East coast). . . . .$ 9,400
    (West coast) . . . .$ 9,489
    in September 1968 (East coast) . . . .$ 9,525
    in October 1969 (East coast). . . . .$ 10,823
    in January 1970 (East coast) . . . .$ 11,327

Production of the 300SEL model [109 E28] (from December 1967/ February 1968 until January 1970)

was in	1967	37 units
	1968	1,325 units
	1969	1,137 units
	1970	20 units
	total	2,519 units

Specifications

	300SEL
Engine type	6 cyl overhead camshaft (M 189)
Bore and stroke	86.5 x 78.8mm (3.41 x 3.10 in)
Displacement	2778 cc (169.5 cu in)
Power output	160 hp (DIN) @ 5500 rpm (180 hp SAE @ 5750 rpm)
Compression ratio	9.5:1
Torque	24.5 mkg @ 4250 rpm (26.7 mkg @ 4500 rpm 193.2 ft/lb)
Fuel injection	Bosch six plunger pump
Engine speed at 100 km/hr	3140 rpm
Gear ratios	I. 3.98:1 II. 2.46:1 III. 1.58:1 IV. 1.00:1
Rear axle ratio	4.08
Chassis	unit frame and body
Suspension	independent front and rear, air springs, self leveling and air suspension, diagonal-pivot swing axle
Brakes and area	disc, servo assisted, 273/279mm (10.8/11.0 in)
Wheelbase	2850mm (112.2 in)
Track, front/rear	1482/1490mm (58.4/58.7 in)
Length	5000mm (196.9 in)
Width	1810mm (71.3 in)
Height	1415mm (55.7 in)
Ground clearance	175mm (6.9 in)
Tires	7.35 H 14 or 185 H 14
Turning circle	12.2 meters (40 ft)
Steering type and ratio	recirculating ball, servo assisted (3.0 turns)
Weight	1620 kg (3564 lbs)
Maximum speed	190 km/hr (118 mph)
Acceleration	11.5 sec 0-100 km/hr
Fuel consumption	12.2 liters/100 km (19 mpg)
Fuel tank capacity	82 liters (21.7 gallons)

Production

Production of the 250C coupe model [114 V25] (from October 1968 until May 1972)

was in	1968	3 units
	1969	2,949 units
	1970	2,627 units
	1971	2,348 units
	1972	897 units
	total	8,824 units

Production of the 250CE model [114 E25] (from October 1968 until May 1972)

was in	1968	3 units
	1969	5,840 units
	1970	8,002 units
	1971	5,898 units
	1972	2,044 units
	total	21,787 units

Production of the 250C model (2,778 cc engine) [114 V28] (from July 1969)

was in	1969	1,213 units
	1970	2,425 units
	1971	3,621 units
	1972	2,839 units
	1973	649 units
	1974	490 units
	1975	442 units
	total	11,679 units

Model 250C (1968-   )

The 250C and 250CE coupe models were introduced toward the end of 1968 as the last of the New Generation cars. The chassis, wheelbase and track, were the same as those of the 250 sedan, but the roof was nearly two inches lower and the passenger compartment was shorter. There were no pillars between the front and rear side windows and the chrome strips on the roof made the car look considerable more sportier than the staid model.

Powered either by the carburetor engine of 130 DIN (146 SAE) horsepower or the electronically controlled fuel injection engine of 150 DIN (170 SAE) horsepower, for the United States the 280 engine was fitted. This developed 157 SAE horsepower and the car had the final drive of 3.92:1 instead of the 4.08 for the former cars. The four-speed manual transmission was optional. Caliper-type disc brakes ensured safe stopping and radial tires provided superb road-holding. The base price of the 250C sporty coupe model, however, at first did not include such extras as air conditioning, automatic transmission, and power steering.

Prices

The 250C coupe sold in 1969 for . . . . .DM	16,820
in 1970 for. . . . . .DM	18,430
in 1971 for. . . . . .DM	19,370
The 250CE coupe sold in 1969 for . . . . .DM	17,710
in 1970 for. . . . . .DM	19,370
in 1971 . . . . .DM	20,370
Power steering . . . . .DM	515
Automatic transmission . . . . .DM	1,440
The 250C (2.8-liter engine) sold in the United States	
in January 1970 for (East coast). . . . .$	6,625
(West coast) . . . .$	6,761
in October 1970 (including automatic transmission)	
(East coast) . . . .$	7,348
in September 1971 (including automatic transmission)	
(East coast) . . . .$	8,059
Power steering (1970) . . . .$	198

Specifications

250C / 250CE (coupe)

Engine type	6 cyl overhead camshaft (M 114) (for U.S. M 130)
Bore and stroke	81.7 x 78.8mm (3.23 x 3.10 in) for U.S.: 86.5 x 78.8mm (3.41 x 3.10 in)
Displacement	2496 cc (152.4 cu in) for U.S.: 2778 cc (169.5 cu in)
Power output	C: 130 hp (DIN) @ 5400 rpm (146 hp SAE @ 5600 rpm) CE: 150 hp (DIN) @ 5500 rpm (170 hp SAE @ 5500 rpm) for U.S.: 157 hp SAE @ 5400
Compression ratio	9:1 (later: 8.7:1)
Torque	C: 20.3 mkg @ 3600 rpm (22.3 mkg @ 3800 rpm 161.3 ft/lb) CE: 21.5 mkg @ 4500 rpm (23.5 mkg @ 4650 rpm 170 ft/lb) for U.S.: 25.1 mkg @ 3800 rpm 181.6 ft/lb
Carburetion or Fuel injection	2 dual downdraft carburetors Zenith 35/40 INAT CE: Bosch electronic
Engine speed at 100 km/hr	3180 rpm
Gear ratios	I. 3.90:1 (optional) I. 3.96:1 II. 2.30:1 II. 2.34:1 III. 1.41:1 III. 1.43:1 IV. 1.00:1 IV. 1.00:1 V. 0.87:1
Rear axle ratio	3.92 (later: 3.69; for 5-speed 3.92)
Chassis	unit frame and body
Suspension	independent front and rear, with coil springs, diagonal-pivot swing axle, anti-sway bars
Brakes and area	disc, power assisted, 273/279mm (10.8/11.0 in)
Wheelbase	2750mm (108.3 in)
Track, front/rear	1444/1440mm (56.9/56.7 in)
Length	4680mm (184.3 in)
Width	1770mm (69.7 in)
Height	1395mm (54.9 in)
Ground clearance	175mm (6.9 in)
Tires	6.95 H 14 or 175 H 14
Turning circle	11.7 meters (38.4 ft)
Steering type and ratio	recirculating ball,(4.0 turns), servo assisted
Weight	1395 kg (3069 lbs)
Maximum speed	180 km/hr (112 mph)
Acceleration	13 sec 0-100 km/hr
Fuel consumption	12.5 liters/100 km (18.75 mpg)
Fuel tank capacity	65 liters (17.2 gallons)

Prices and Production

The 280SE 3.5 coupe sold in 1970 for. . . . . .DM 32,025
    in 1971 for. . . . . .DM 33,690
The 280SE 3.5 convertible sold for an additional about DM 2,000
The 280SE 3.5 coupe sold in the United States
    in January 1970 for (East coast). . . . .$ 13,430
    (West coast) . . . .$ 13,574
    in March 1971 (East coast) . . . .$ 13,766
The 280SE 3.5 convertible sold in the United States
    in January 1970 for (East coast). . . . .$ 14,155
    (West coast) . . . .$ 14,297
    in March 1971 (East coast) . . . .$ 14,509

Production of the 280SE 3.5 [111 E35/1] (from August/November
1969 until July 1971)

was in	1969	176 units
	1970	3,300 units
	1971	1,026 units
	total	4,502 units

Model 280SE 3.5 (1969-1971)

    The 280SE 3.5 luxury coupe and convertible were introduced at the Frankfurt Auto Show in 1969. The basic body style actually dated back to the 1961 220SE model, and it was only slightly altered. The radiator was 70 millimeters lower and 100 millimeters wider and the bumpers had rubber inserts. The engine, however, was the most advanced one produced, with transistorized ignition, three-phase generator, and Bosch electronic fuel injection. Such accessories as stereo radio, air conditioning, automatic transmission, and electric windows were standard. Upholstery was of real leather and the elegant wood trim was especially selected.

    The new V-8 engine, displacing 3,499 cubic centimeters (213.5 cubic inches), and developing 200 horsepower (230 SAE) was brand-new and did not share any components with the earlier and larger 6.3-liter unit. With the cast-iron block and aluminum head, it weighed only 55 pounds more (505 pounds) than the six-cylinder powerplant and gave the cars an acceleration rate of 9.5 seconds to 100 kilometers per hour and maximum speed of 125 miles per hour.

Specifications

	280SE 3.5 (coupe and convertible)
Engine type	V-8 cyl overhead camshafts, one for each bank (M 116)
Bore and stroke	92 x 65.8mm (3.62 x 2.59 in)
Displacement	3499 cc (213.5 cu in)
Power output	200 hp (DIN) @ 5800 rpm (230 hp SAE @ 6050 rpm)
Compression ratio	9.5:1
Torque	29.2 mkg @ 4000 rpm (32 mkg @ 4200 rpm 231.5 ft/lb)
Fuel injection	Bosch electronic
Engine speed at 100 km/hr	2945 rpm
Gear ratios	I. 3.98:1 (14.69) II. 2.39:1 (8.82) III. 1.46:1 (5.38) IV. 1.00:1 (3.69)
Rear axle ratio	3.69
Chassis	unit frame and body
Suspension	independent front and rear, with coil springs, single joint swing axle
Brakes and area	disc, servo assist, two circuit hydraulic, 273/279mm (10.8/11.0 in)
Wheelbase	2750mm (108.3 in)
Track, front/rear	1482/1485mm (58.4/58.6 in)
Length	4880mm (192 in)
Width	1845mm (72.6 in)
Height	1395mm (54.9 in)
Ground clearance	152mm (6 in)
Tires	7.35 H 14 or 185 H 14
Turning circle	12 meters (39.4 ft)
Steering type and ratio	recirculating ball (3.2 turns), servo assisted
Weight	convertible: 1574 kg (3463 lbs); coupe: 1655 kg (3641 lbs)
Maximum speed	205 km/hr (127 mph)
Acceleration	9.5 sec 0-100 km/hr
Fuel consumption	13 liters, super/100 km (18 mpg)
Fuel tank capacity	82 liters (21.7 gallons)

Model 300SEL 3.5 (1969-1972)

The 300SEL 3.5 sedan was the other car introduced at the 1969 Frankfurt Auto Show to have the new V-8 engine of 3.5-liter displacement installed. The body style was identical to the earlier 300SEL sedan which had the 6-cylinder-in-line engine of 2.8 liters and 180 SAE (160 DIN) horsepower. This, in turn, had replaced the first 300SEL sedan which actually had a 300 engine, the 2,996 cubic centimeter power unit of 160, and later 170 (DIN) horsepower.

The new 300SEL 3.5 was again the top of the line, a most luxuriously appointed automobile, more advanced than the coming 280SE 3.5 sedan in chassis design, and, with the longer wheelbase, a somewhat better riding automobile. It had the air suspension system of the 6.3 model sedan and shared some other technological improvements of that model.

Prices and Production

The 300SEL 3.5 four-door sedan sold in 1970 for . . . . .DM 31,025
    in 1971 for. . . . . .DM 32,635
The 300SEL 3.5 four-door sedan sold in the United States
    in January 1970 for (East coast). . . . .$ 12,572
       (West coast) . . . .$ 12,718
    in March 1971 (East coast) . . . .$ 12,886
    in September 1971 (East coast) . . . .$ 14,121
    in December 1971 (East coast). . . . .$ 13,768

Production of the 300SEL 3.5 model [109 E35/1] (from August/November 1969 until September 1972)

was in	1969	158 units
	1970	4,903 units
	1971	3,225 units
	1972	1,297 units
total		9,483 units

Specifications

	300SEL 3.5
Engine type	V-8 cyl overhead camshafts, one for each bank (M 116)
Bore and stroke	92 x 65.8mm (3.62 x 2.59 in)
Displacement	3499 cc (213.5 cu in)
Power output	200 hp (DIN) @ 5800 rpm (230 hp SAE @ 6050 rpm)
Compression ratio	9.5:1
Torque	29.2 mkg @ 4000 rpm (32 mkg @ 4200 rpm 231.5 ft/lb)
Fuel injection	Bosch electronic
Engine speed at 100 km/hr	2945 rpm
Gear ratios	I. 3.98:1 (14.69) II. 2.39:1 (8.82) III. 1.46:1 (5.38) IV. 1.00:1 (3.69)
Rear axle ratio	3.69
Chassis	unit frame and body
Suspension	independent front and rear, air springs, self leveling and air suspension, diagonal swing axle
Brakes and area	front vented disc, rear solid, servo assisted, 273/279mm (10.8/11.0 in)
Wheelbase	2850mm (112.2 in)
Track, front/rear	1482/1490mm (58.4/58.7 in)
Length	5000mm (196.9 in)
Width	1810mm (71.3 in)
Height	1415mm (55.7 in)
Ground clearance	175mm (6.9 in)
Tires	7.35 H 14 or 185 H 14
Turning circle	12.2 meters (40 ft)
Steering type and ratio	recirculating ball (3.0 turns), servo assisted
Weight	1673 kg (3680 lbs)
Maximum speed	205 km/hr (127 mph)
Acceleration	9.5 sec 0-100 km/hr
Fuel consumption	13 liters, super/100 km (18 mpg)
Fuel tank capacity	82 liters (21.7 gallons)

Prices and Production

The 250 four-door sedan sold in 1970 for . . . . .DM 16,185
    in 1972 for. . . . . .DM 17,875
    in 1973 for. . . . . .DM 18,760
The 250 four-door sedan sold in the United States
    in January 1970 for (East coast). . . . .$ 5,539
      (West coast) . . . .$ 5,674
    in October 1970 (including automatic transmission)
      (East coast) . . . .$ 6,208
    in September 1971 (including automatic transmission)
      (East coast) . . . .$ 7,205
    Power steering (1970) . . . .$ 198

Production of the 250 model [114 V28] (from March/July 1970)
            was in 1970   3,248 units
                   1971   7,382 units
                   1972   8,266 units
                   1973   6,570 units
                   1974   4,516 units
                   1975   3,580 units
                           ————————
               total   33,562 units

Model 250 (1970-   )

The 250 sedan, first produced March and placed into regular production in July 1970, was another model where the designation no longer indicated the displacement of the engine, for it had the 2,778 cubic centimeter engine. The true 250 was still being made (begun in July and put into production in December 1967, it was phased out in May 1972). After the appearance of the 2.8-liter 250 coupe the previous year, the 2.8-liter sedan was probably a natural 250 model to follow.

Sharing the body style of the larger 280SEL sedan, the 250 was shorter, had a smaller fuel tank, smaller sized tires, weighed 178 pounds less, but had the same specifications in other respects. In actual performance it was slightly superior to the larger sedan.

Specifications

	250
Engine type	6 cyl overhead camshaft (M 114)
Bore and stroke	86.5 x 78.8mm (3.41 x 3.10 in)
Displacement	2778 cc (169.5 cu in)
Power output	140 hp (DIN) @ 5200 rpm (157 hp SAE @ 5400 rpm)
Compression ratio	9:1
Torque	23 mkg @ 3600 rpm (25.1 mkg @ 3800 rpm 181.6 ft/lb)
Carburetion	2 dual downdraft carburetors Zenith 35/40 INAT
Engine speed at 100 km/hr	3140 rpm
Gear ratio	I. 3.90:1 II. 2.30:1 III. 1.41:1 IV. 1.00:1
Rear axle ratio	3.92
Chassis	unit frame and body
Suspension	independent front and rear, with coil springs, diagonal-pivot swing axle, anti-sway bars
Brakes and area	disc, power assist, two circuit hydraulic, 273/279mm (10.8/11.0 in)
Wheelbase	2750mm (108.3 in)
Track, front/rear	1444/1440mm (56.9/56.7 in)
Length	4680mm (184.3 in)
Width	1770mm (69.7 in)
Height	1440mm (56.7 in)
Ground clearance	175mm (6.9 in)
Tires	6.95 H 14
Turning circle	11.7 meters (38.4 ft)
Steering type and ratio	recirculating ball (4.0 turns), servo assisted
Weight	1445 kg (3179 lbs)
Maximum speed	190 km/hr (118 mph)
Acceleration	12 sec 0-100 km/hr
Fuel consumption	12.5 liters, super/100 km (18.75 mpg)
Fuel tank capacity	65 liters (17.2 gallons)

Model 280SEL 3.5 (1970-1972)

The 280SEL 3.5 sedan introduced at the Auto Show in Amsterdam, was produced for only three years. First pre-production was begun in June 1970 with only three units being built that year. Regular production did not get underway until the following March. After placing that 3.5-liter V-8 engine into the luxury coupe and convertible of the 280SE line, it seemed only natural to equip the sedan in the same manner. However, the 300SEL sedan, a more elegant model, was already in production and selling in fair numbers, even when the less expensive 280SEL was available. (The 300SEL 3.5 sold nearly 9,500 units in four years, while the 280SEL 3.5 sold less than 1,000 units in two years.)

Prices and Production

The 280SEL 3.5 four-door sedan sold in 1971 for . . . . .DM 31,420
In the United States the 280SEL 3.5 sedan sold
  in 1970 for (including automatic transmission)
  (East coast) . . . .$ 8,088
  (West coast) . . . .$ 8,259
  in September 1971 (including automatic transmission)
  (East coast) . . . .$ 10,925
  in December 1971 (including automatic transmission)
  (East coast) . . . .$ 10,634
Power steering (1970) . . . .$ 198

Production of the 280SEL 3.5 model [108 E35] (from June 1970/
March 1971 until August 1972)

	was in	1970	3 units
		1971	565 units
		1972	383 units
		total	951 units

Specifications

	280SEL 3.5
Engine type	V-8 cyl overhead camshafts, one for each bank (M 116)
Bore and stroke	92 x 65.8mm (3.62 x 2.59 in)
Displacement	3499 cc (213.5 cu in)
Power output	200 hp (DIN) @ 5800 rpm (230 hp SAE @ 6050 rpm)
Compression ratio	9.5:1
Torque	29.2 mkg @ 4000 rpm (32 mkg @ 4200 rpm 231.5 ft/lb)
Fuel injection	Bosch electronic
Engine speed at 100 km/hr	2945 rpm
Gear ratios	I. 3.98:1 II. 2.39:1 III. 1.46:1 IV. 1.00:1
Rear axle ratio	3.69
Chassis	unit frame and body
Suspension	independent front and rear, with coil springs, diagonal-pivot swing axle, anti-sway bars
Brakes and area	front vented disc, rear solid, servo assisted, two circuit hydraulic, 273/279mm (10.8/11.0 in)
Wheelbase	2850mm (112.2 in)
Track, front/rear	1482/1490mm (58.4/58.7 in)
Length	4780mm (188.2 in)
Width	1770mm (69.7 in)
Height	1440mm (56.7 in)
Ground clearance	175mm (6.9 in)
Tires	7.35 H 14 or 185 H 14
Turning circle	12.2 meters (40 ft)
Steering type and ratio	recirculating ball (4.0 turns), servo assisted
Weight	1762 kg (3876 lbs)
Maximum speed	200 km/hr (124 mph)
Acceleration	10 sec 0-100 km/hr
Fuel consumption	13 liters, super/100 km (18 mpg)
Fuel tank capacity	82 liters, (21.7 gallons)

Model 280SE 3.5 (1970-1972)

The 280SE 3.5 sedan, first produced in July 1970, but really not in regular series production until March of the following year, was a more powerful edition of the prevailing sedan model. The new V-type eight-cylinder engine had been first installed into the higher priced luxury coupe and convertible models and the longer wheelbase sedans of the 280SEL and 300SEL designation. It seemed natural to make that better performance car also available in the regular sedan style.

Still, the 280SE 3.5 sedan had a relatively short production run with slightly over 11,000 units in two years. It was then replaced by the more correctly named model and with the newer styled body and other notable improvements gained over the years.

Prices and Production

The 280SE 3.5 four-door sedan sold in 1971 for . . . . . .DM 24,920
In the United States the 280SE 3.5 sedan sold
  in 1970 for (including automatic transmission)
  (East coast) . . . .$ 7,297
  (West coast) . . . .$ 7,461
  in September 1971 (including automatic transmission)
  (East coast) . . . .$ 9,546
  in December 1971 (including automatic transmission)
  (East coast) . . . .$ 9,503
Power steering (1970) . . . .$ 198

Production of the 280SE 3.5 model [108 E35] (from July 1970/
March 1971 until September 1972)

	was in	1970	3 units
		1971	7,450 units
		1972	3,856 units
		total	11,309 units

Specifications

	280SE 3.5
Engine type	V-8 cyl overhead camshafts (M 116)
Bore and stroke	92 x 65.8mm (3.62 x 2.59 in)
Displacement	3499 cc (213.5 cu in)
Power output	200 hp (DIN) @ 5800 rpm (230 hp SAE @ 6050 rpm)
Compression ratio	9.5:1
Torque	29.2 mkg @ 4000 rpm (32 mkg @ 4200 rpm 231.5 ft/lb)
Fuel injection	Bosch electronic
Engine speed at 100 km/hr	2945 rpm
Gear ratios	I. 3.98:1 II. 2.39:1 III. 1.46:1 IV. 1.00:1
Rear axle ratio	3.69
Chassis	unit frame and body
Suspension	independent front and rear, with coil springs, diagonal-pivot swing axle, anti-sway bars
Brakes and area	disc, front vented, rear solid, servo assisted, two circuit hydraulic, 273/279mm (10.8/11.0 in)
Wheelbase	2750mm (108.3 in)
Track, front/rear	1482/1490mm (58.4/58.7 in)
Length	4680mm (184.3 in)
Width	1770mm (69.7 in)
Height	1440mm (56.7 in)
Ground clearance	175mm (6.9 in)
Tires	7.35 H 14 or 185 H 14
Turning circle	11.7 meters (38.4 ft)
Steering type and ratio	recirculating ball (4.0 turns), servo assisted
Weight	1737 kg (3821 lbs)
Maximum speed	200 km/hr (124 mph)
Acceleration	10 sec 0-100 km/hr
Fuel consumption	13 liters, super/100 km (18 mpg)
Fuel tank capacity	82 liters (21.7 gallons)

Prices and Production

The 350SL model sold in 1971 for . . . . .DM 29,970
   in 1972 for. . . . . .DM 31,415
   in 1973 for. . . . . .DM 32,915
   in 1974 for. . . . . .DM 34,400
   in 1975 for. . . . . .DM 37,920
In the United States the 350SL sold
   in September 1971 for (East coast). . . . .$ 11,059
   in December 1971 for (East coast) . . . .$ 10,540

Production of the 350SL model [107 E35] (from November 1970/
April 1971)

	was in	1970	3 units
		1971	4,802 units
		1972	4,778 units
		1973	1,647 units
		1974	574 units
		1975	390 units
		total	12,194 units

Model 350SL (1970-   )

The 350SL model was introduced early in 1971, although the preproduction actually got started in November of the previous year. The impressive two-seater sports car was to replace the 280SL, which had actually started with the 230SL version in 1963. The body and chassis of this all-new car was considerably heavier (300 lbs.) and longer (3.3 in.) than that of the earlier sportscars, but still showed a slight resemblance to them. The front and rear axles were similar to those of the 200-250 models, with independent wheel suspension with double wishbones and anti-drive control at the front, diagonal swing axle at the rear. The steel coil springs had rubber helping springs, anti-roll bars, and double-acting hydraulic telescopic shock absorbers. Brakes were ventilated disc at front and solid on the rear, hydraulic dual circuit with vacuum boost. A fluid-coupling four-speed automatic transmission was available as an optional item. Some of the many new safety features of the 350SL were the four-spoke safety steering wheel, the fuel tank repositioned, collision-safe over the rear axle, the safety door handles, and a new type safety belt.

The engine was the 3.5-liter V-8 type with slight modifications from those of the other 3.5 models. The gear shift lever was placed on the floor and the regular four-speed transmission or automatic was available. Maximum speed was 210 km/hr and acceleration was 8.8 seconds to 100 kilometers per hour, with the standard transmission car.

The car came as an open roadster with removable hard top pagoda style roof.

The 350SL 4.5 was marketed in the U.S. It was the same car with few exceptions, but had the larger 4.5-liter engine installed. Rated at the same horsepower as the European version (3.5) the larger engine used 10 percent more fuel, but regular instead of super gasoline. Emission controls were met until 1974 with the 4.5 — the principal reason for the change to a larger displacement engine for the U.S.

Specifications

	350SL					
Engine type	V-8 overhead camshafts (M 116)					
Bore and stroke	92 x 65.8mm (3.62 x 2.59 in)					
Displacement	3499 cc (213.5 cu in)					
Power output	200 hp (DIN) @ 5800 rpm (230 hp SAE @ 6050 rpm)					
Compression ratio	9.5:1					
Torque	29.2 mkg @ 4000 rpm (32 mkg @ 4200 rpm 231.5 ft/lb)					
Fuel injection	Bosch electronic					
Engine speed at 100 km/hr	2945 rpm					
Gear ratios	I. 3.98:1	automatic	I. 3.96:1	after July, 1972	I. 2.31:1	
	II. 2.39:1		II. 2.34:1		II. 1.46:1	
	III. 1.46:1		III. 1.43:1		III. 1.00:1	
	IV. 1.00:1		IV. 1.00:1			
Rear axle ratio	3.46					
Chassis	unit frame and body					
Suspension	independent front and rear, double wishbones, diagonal-pivot swing axle					
Brakes and area	disc, front vented, rear solid, 278/279mm (10.9/11.0 in)					
Wheelbase	2460mm (96.9 in)					
Track, front/rear	1452/1440mm (57.2/56.7 in)					
Length	4380mm (172.4 in)					
Width	1790mm (70.5 in)					
Height	1300mm (51.2 in)					
Ground clearance	140mm (5.5 in)					
Tires	205/70 VR 14					
Turning circle	10.34 meters (33.9 ft)					
Steering type and ratio	recirculating ball (3.0 turns); servo assisted 15.6:1					
Weight	1585 kg (3487 lbs)					
Maximum speed	210 km/hr (130 mph); automatic: 205 km/hr (127 mph)					
Accleration	8.8 sec 0-100 km/hr; automatic: 9.0 sec 0-100 km/hr					
Fuel consumption	13 liters, super/100 km (18 mpg)					
Fuel tank capacity	90 liters (23 gallons)					

Prices and Production

The 350SLC model sold in 1971 for . . . . .DM 33,690
in 1972 for. . . . . .DM 35,635
in 1973 for. . . . . .DM 37,300
in 1974 for. . . . . .DM 38,980
in 1975 for. . . . . .DM 42,970

Production of the 350SLC model [107 E35] (from June 1971/
February 1972)

was in	1971	6 units
	1972	5,562 units
	1973	3,750 units
	1974	864 units
	1975	589 units
	total	10,771 units

Model 350SLC (1971-   )

The 350SLC model was first shown to the public at the Brussels Auto Show in 1971. It was a slightly longer edition of the SL model. The wheelbase as well as overall length was 360 millimeter (about 14 inches) longer and the car weighed 50 kilograms more. The coupe had, of course, rear passenger seats and larger trunk space than the 350SL model, but it looked just like it except for the short space of louvered rear side window area.

This newly designed luxury coupe took the place of the (111 factory designation) line of coupes and convertibles first produced as 220SE in September 1960 and followed by the steadily increased power of the 250SE and 280SE models.

It was over six inches shorter and three inches lower than the older body style car.

The 350SLC was an automobile with the sporty character of the SL model, giving superior performance, exclusive comfort, and elegant styling to the discriminating owner. Fitted with the four-speed manual or automatic transmission, the SLC had the same performance as the SL model.

For the United States, the 195 horsepower (DIN) 4.5-liter engine was installed and only the three-speed automatic transmission was available. Many items were standard equipment, such as air conditioning, automatic transmission, power brakes, power steering, central locking system, stereo radio, leather upholstery, and Michelin XVR tires, among others.

Specifications

	350SLC
Engine type	V-8 cyl overhead camshafts (M 116)
Bore and stroke	92 x 65.8mm (3.62 x 2.59 in)
Displacement	3499 cc (213.5 cu in)
Power output	200 hp (DIN) @ 5800 rpm (230 hp SAE @ 6050 rpm)
Compression ratio	9.5:1
Torque	29.2 mkg @ 4000 rpm (32 mkg @ 4200 rpm 231.5 ft/lb)
Fuel injection	Bosch electronic
Engine speed at 100 km/hr	2945 rpm
Gear ratios	I. 3.98:1 automatic I. 3.96:1 after July, 1972 I. 2.31:1 II. 2.39:1 II. 2.34:1 II. 1.46:1 III. 1.46:1 III. 1.43:1 III. 1.00:1 IV. 1.00:1 IV. 1.00:1
Rear axle ratio	3.64
Chassis	unit frame and body
Suspension	independent front and rear, double wishbones, diagonal swing axle
Brakes and area	disc, front vented, rear solid, 278/279mm (10.9/11.0 in)
Wheelbase	2820mm (111.0 in)
Track, front/rear	1452/1440mm (57.2/56.7 in)
Length	4740mm (186.6 in)
Width	1790mm (70.5 in)
Height	1300mm (51.2 in)
Ground clearance	140mm (5.5 in)
Tires	205/70 VR
Turning circle	10.34 meters (33.9 ft)
Steering type and ratio	recirculating ball (3.0 turns); servo assisted 15.6:1
Weight	1635 kg (3597 lbs)
Maximum speed	210 km/hr (130 mph); automatic: 205 km/hr (127 mph)
Acceleration	8.8 sec 0-100 km/hr; automatic: 9.0 sec 0-100 km/hr
Fuel consumption	13 liters, super/100 km (18 mpg)
Fuel tank capacity	90 liters (23 gallons)

Model 280 (1971-   )

The 280 sedan, fitted with the newly developed six-cylinder engine with two overhead camshafts, was introduced in early 1972. The design of an altered shape of combustion chamber and different positioning of valves and double camshafts made for more complete burning of fuel and less emission of noxious exhaust gases (15 percent less hydrocarbon and 10 percent less carbon monoxide) and was an answer to the ever-increasing stringent emission controls.

Equipped with the dual downdraft Solex carburetor, The M110 engine developed 160 DIN horsepower at 5,500 revolutions per minute and 23 mkg torque at 4,000. The new sedan came equipped with the all-synchromesh four-speed transmission with steering column or center floor gear shift, but had the manual five-speed transmission or the automatic unit as an optional item. It was a larger version of the 250 sedan.

Prices and Production

The 280 four-door sedan sold in 1972 for . . . . .DM 18,980
   in 1973 for. . . . . .DM 19,925
   in 1974 for. . . . . .DM 21,700
   in 1975 for. . . . . .DM 23,610
   Power steering . . . . .DM   515
   Automatic transmission . . . . .DM 1,440
In the United States the 280 sedan sold in 1972 for
   (including automatic transmission)
     (East coast) . . . .$ 8,875
     (West coast) . . . .$ 8,978
   in November 1973 (East coast) . . . .$ 10,950
   in September 1974 (East coast) . . . .$ 12,325
   in October 1975 (East coast) . . . .$ 13,813

Production of the 280 model [114 V28] (from October 1971/May 1972)

	was in	1971	2 units
		1972	9,828 units
		1973	13,718 units
		1974	11,755 units
		1975	6,535 units
		total	41,838 units

Specifications

	280
Engine type	6 cyl double overhead camshafts (M 110)
Bore and stroke	86 x 78.8mm (3.41 x 3.10 in)
Displacement	2746 cc (168 cu in)
Power output	160 hp (DIN) @ 5500 rpm (180 hp SAE) later, U.S.: 120 hp SAE @ 4800 rpm
Compression ratio	9:1 (U.S.: 8:1)
Torque	23 mkg @ 4000 rpm (166.4 ft/lb)
Carburetion	dual downdraft carburetor Solex 4 A 1
Engine speed at 100 km/hr	3140 rpm
Gear ratios	I. 3.90:1 II. 2.30:1 III. 1.41:1 IV. 1.00:1
Rear axle ratio	3.69
Chassis	unit frame and body
Suspension	independent front and rear, with coil springs, diagonal-pivot swing axle, anti-sway bars
Brakes and area	disc, power assisted, two circuit hydraulic, 273/279mm (10.8/11.0 in)
Wheelbase	2750mm (108.3 in)
Track, front/rear	1444/1440mm (56.9/56.7 in)
Length	4680mm (184.3 in)
Width	1770mm (69.7 in)
Height	1440mm (56.7 in)
Ground clearance	175mm (6.9 in)
Tires	185 HR 14
Turning circle	11.7 meters (38.4 ft)
Steering type and ratio	recirculating ball (4.0 turns), servo assisted
Weight	1455 kg (3200 lbs)
Maximum speed	190 km/hr (118 mph)
Acceleration	13 sec 0-100 km/hr (18.75 mpg)
Fuel consumption	12.5 liters, super/100 km (later, U.S.: no lead fuel)
Fuel tank capacity	65 liters (17.2 gallons)

Model 280E (1971-)

The 280E sedan introduced in early 1971, but not produced in any quantity until the following year, had the new double overhead camshaft six-cylinder engine, but with electronic fuel enjection. This version of the M110 engine developed 185 DIN horsepower at 6,000 revolutions per minute and 24.3 mkg torque at 4,500 revolutions. Performance was slightly better than that of the carburetor model, with maximum speed of 200 kilometers (124 miles) against the 190 of the 280 sedan, but fuel consumption was rated equal.

Inside furnishing was exactly the same and so was the exterior body style except for the designation E on the trunk lid after the 280.

Prices and Production

The 280E four-door sedan sold in 1972 for . . . . .DM 20,535
    in 1973 for. . . . . .DM 21,535
    in 1974 for. . . . . .DM 22,500
    in 1975 for. . . . . .DM 25,465
    Power steering . . . . .DM   515
    Automatic transmission . . . . .DM 1,440

Production of the 280E model [114 E28] (from January 1971/
April 1972)

was in	1971	18 units
	1972	8,371 units
	1973	8,214 units
	1974	3,612 units
	1975	2,277 units
	total	22,492 units

Specifications

	280E
Engine type	6 cyl double overhead camshafts (M 110)
Bore and stroke	86 x 78.8mm (3.41 x 3.10 in)
Displacement	2746 cc (168 cu in)
Power output	185 hp (DIN) @ 6000 rpm (205 hp SAE)
Compression ratio	9:1
Torque	24.3 mkg @ 4500 rpm (175.8 ft/lb)
Fuel injection	Bosch electronic
Engine speed at 100 km/hr	3140 rpm
Gear ratios	I. 3.90:1 II. 2.30:1 III. 1.41:1 IV. 1.00:1
Rear axle ratio	3.69
Chassis	unit frame and body
Suspension	independent front and rear, with coil springs, diagonal-pivot swing axle, anti-sway bars
Brakes and area	disc, power assisted, two circuit hydraulic, 273/279mm (10.8/11.0 in)
Wheelbase	2750mm (108.3 in)
Track, front/rear	1444/1440mm (56.9/56.7 in)
Length	4680mm (184.3 in)
Width	1770mm (69.7 in)
Height	1440mm (56.7 in)
Ground clearance	175mm (6.9 in)
Tires	185 HR 14
Turning circle	11.7 meters (38.4 ft)
Steering type and ratio	recirculating ball (4.0 turns), servo assisted
Weight	1455 kg (3200 lbs)
Maximum speed	200 km/hr (124 mph)
Acceleration	12 sec 0-100 km/hr
Fuel consumption	12.5 liters, super/100 km (18.75 mpg)
Fuel tank capacity	65 liters (17.2 gallons)

Model 280C (1971-   )

The 280C coupe appeared on the scene in early 1972. It had been originated in the late period of the previous year, along with the sedan line, and one car was actually produced in December 1971. The new double overhead camshaft six-cylinder engine, equipped with the Solex dual compound downdraft carburetor, was fitted into the coupe body of the 250C model. Specifications, except for the new engine installation, were the same as those of the previous model, which remained in production.

Prices and Production

The 280C coupe sold in 1972 for . . . . .DM	21,425
in 1973 for. . . . . .DM	22,480
in 1974 for. . . . . .DM	24,500
in 1975 for. . . . . .DM	26,555
Power steering . . . . .DM	515
Automatic transmission . . . . .DM	1,440

In the United States the 280C coupe sold

in September 1972 for (East coast). . . . .$	9,518
(West coast) . . . .$	9,618
in November 1973 (East coast) . . . .$	11,630
in September 1974 (East coast) . . . .$	13,063
in October 1975 (East coast). . . . .$	14,639

Production of the 280C coupe [114 V28] (from December 1971/ June 1972)

was in	1971	1 unit
	1972	2,124 units
	1973	4,196 units
	1974	3,734 units
	1975	2,133 units
	total	12,188 units

Specifications

	280C (coupe)
Engine type	6 cyl double overhead camshafts (M 110)
Bore and stroke	86 x 78.8mm (3.41 x 3.10 in)
Displacement	2746 cc (168 cu in)
Power output	160 hp (DIN) @ 5500 rpm (180 hp SAE) later, U.S.: 120 hp SAE @ 4800 rpm; 1975 California: 123 hp SAE @ 5000 rpm
Compression ratio	9:1 (U.S.: 8:1)
Torque	23 mkg @ 4000 rom (166.4 ft/lb) later, U.S.: 15.5 mkg @ 2800 rpm (120 ft/lb); 1975: 143 ft/lb @ 2800 rpm California: 143 ft/lb @ 3600 rpm
Carburetion	dual downdraft carburetors Solex 4 A 1
Engine speed at 100 km/hr	3140 rpm
Gear ratios	I. 3.90:1 optional I. 3.96:1 II. 2.30:1 II. 2.34:1 III. 1.41:1 III. 1.43:1 IV. 1.00:1 IV. 1.00:1 V. 0.87:1
Rear axle ratio	3.69 (for 5-speed 3.92)
Chassis	unit frame and body
Suspension	independent front and rear, with coil springs, diagonal-pivot swing axle, anti-sway bars
Brakes and area	disc, power assisted, 273/279mm (10.8/11.0 in)
Wheelbase	2750mm (108.3 in)
Track, front/rear	1444/1440mm (56.9/56.7 in)
Length	4680mm (184.5 in)
Width	1770mm (69.7 in)
Height	1395mm (54.9 in)
Ground clearance	175mm (6.9 in)
Tires	185 HR 14
Turning circle	11.7 meters (38.4 ft)
Steering type and ratio	recirculating ball (4.0 turns), servo assisted
Weight	1455 kg (3200 lbs)
Maximum speed	190 km/hr (118 mph)
Acceleration	13 sec 0-100 km/hr (18.75 mpg)
Fuel consumption	12.5 liters, super/100 km (U.S.: no lead fuel)
Fuel tank capacity	65 liters (17.2 gallons)

Model 280CE (1971-   )

The 280CE coupe was introduced at about the same time to the general public as the carburetor version of the car, but pre-production had actually begun in April of 1971. At that time, however, only two prototypes were made and production did not get underway until 1972 when over five thousand units of this double overhead camshaft engined model were built. The electronic fuel injected version developed 185 DIN horsepower at 6,000 revolutions per minute and a torque of 24.3 mkg at 4,500 revolutions per minute, giving the coupe a considerably livelier performance than the carburetor engined model.

Prices and Production

The 280CE sold in 1972 for	DM 22,980
in 1973 for	DM 24,090
in 1974 for	DM 26,240
in 1975 for	DM 28,405
Power steering	DM 515
Automatic transmission	DM 1,440

Production of the 280CE coupe [114 E28] (from April 1971/ May 1972)

was in	1971	2 units
	1972	5,389 units
	1973	3,724 units
	1974	1,429 units
	1975	844 units
	total	11,388 units

Specifications

	280CE (coupe)
Engine type	6 cyl double overhead camshafts (M 110)
Bore and stroke	86 x 78.8mm (3.41 x 3.10 in)
Displacement	2746 cc (168 cu in)
Power output	185 hp (DIN) @ 6000 rpm (205 hp SAE)
Compression ratio	9:1
Torque	24.3 mkg @ 4500 rpm (175.8 ft/lb)
Fuel injection	Bosch electronic
Engine speed at 100 km/hr	3140 rpm
Gear ratios	I. 3.90:1 optional I. 3.96:1 II. 2.30:1 II. 2.34:1 III. 1.41:1 III. 1.43:1 IV. 1.00:1 IV. 1.00:1 V. 0.87:1
Rear axle ratio	3.69 (for 5-speed 3.82)
Chassis	unit frame and body
Suspension	independent front and rear, with coil springs, diagonal-pivot swing axle, anti-sway bars
Brakes and area	disc, power assisted, 273/279mm (10.8/11.0 in)
Wheelbase	2750mm (108.3 in)
Track, front/rear	1444/1440mm (56.9/56.7 in)
Length	4680mm (184.5 in)
Width	1770mm (69.7 in)
Height	1395mm (54.9 in)
Ground clearance	175mm (6.9 in)
Tires	185 HR 14
Turning circle	11.7 meters (38.4 ft)
Steering type and ratio	recirculating ball (4.0 turns), servo assisted
Weight	1455 kg (3200 lbs)
Maximum speed	200 km/hr (124 mph)
Acceleration	12 sec 0-100 km/hr
Fuel consumption	12.5 liters, super/100km (18.75 mpg)
Fuel tank capacity	65 liters (17.2 gallons)

Model 280SE 4.5 (1971-1972)

The 280SE 4.5 sedan made its first appearance in early 1971, just a few months after the new 4.5-liter V-8 engine had made its debut. In fact, that model was available to the purchaser at about the same time the 3.5-liter engined sedan was produced, and gave the buyer another option in power for his car. It was, however, not the choice of as many buyers as was the 3.5-liter engined sedan the first year of production when nearly 6,000 units were sold, but the following year it outsold the smaller-engined version by a margin of two to one.

Inside and out, the two sedans were alike, with the more powerful one having, of course, better performance. Acceleration was slightly faster and the maximum speed was five miles better, but fuel consumption was 1.5 liters more for the 4.5- than for the 3.5-liter engined sedan.

The 280SE 4.5 sedan fitted into the policy of offering the customer the widest possible range in passenger automobiles.

Prices and Production

In the United Stated the 280SE 4.5 sedan sold
in September 1972 for (East coast)............$ 10,283
(West coast) . . . .$ 10,393

Production of the 280SE 4.5 model [108 E45] (from April/May 1971 until November 1972)

	was in	1971	5,782 units
		1972	7,745 units
		total	13,527 units

Specifications

	280SE 4.5
Engine type	V-8 cyl overhead camshafts (M 117)
Bore and stroke	92 x 85mm (3.62 x 3.35 in)
Displacement	4520 cc (275.8 cu in)
Power output	225 hp (DIN) @ 5000 rpm (250 hp SAE) U.S.: 230 hp SAE @ 5000 rpm
Compression ratio	8.8:1 U.S.: 8:1
Torque	38.5 mkg @ 3000 rpm (278.5 ft/lb)
Fuel injection	Bosch electronic
Engine speed at 100 km/hr	2865 rpm U.S.: 2740 rpm
Gear ratios	I. 3.98:1 U.S. automatic I. 2.31:1 II. 2.39:1 II. 1.46:1 III. 1.46:1 III. 1.00:1 IV. 1.00:1
Rear axle ratio	3.69 U.S.: 3.23
Chassis	unit frame and body
Suspension	independent front and rear, with coil springs, diagonal-pivot swing axle, anti-sway bars
Brakes and area	disc, front and rear vented, servo assisted, two circuit hydraulic, 273/279mm (10.8/11.0 in)
Wheelbase	2750mm (108.3 in)
Track, front/rear	1482/1490mm (58.4/58.7 in)
Length	4680mm (184.3 in)
Width	1770mm (69.7 in)
Height	1440mm (56.7 in)
Ground clearance	175mm (6.9 in)
Tires	735 H 14 or 185 H 14
Turning circle	11.7 meters (38.4 ft)
Steering type and ratio	recirculating ball (4.0 turns), servo assisted
Weight	1737 kg (3821 lbs)
Maximum speed	205 km/hr (127 mph) U.S.: 190 km/hr (118 mph)
Acceleration	9.5 sec 0-100 km/hr U.S.: 12 sec 0-100 km/hr
Fuel consumption	14.5 liters, super/100 km (16 mpg)
Fuel tank capacity	82 liters (21.7 gallons)

Model 280SEL 4.5 (1971-1972)

The 280SEL 4.5 sedan was produced at about the same time (in 1971) the regular length sedan was available. Again, this longer wheelbase car was identical to the other model, and the extra ten centimeters gave the rear-seat passengers additional space to stretch their legs. On longer journeys this was especially appreciated.

This 4.5-liter engined long sedan outsold the 3.5-liter version by about three to one during the first year of its availability and the following year this more powerful version was the choice of over 6,000 customers while only about 500 bought the less powerful car. Apparently the extra fuel consumption was of no serious concern to the buyers of the 4.5-liter long sedan.

Prices and Production

In the United States the 280SEL 4.5 sedan sold
in September 1972 for (East coast). . . . .$ 10,875
    (West coast) . . . .$ 10,985

Production of the 280SEL 4.5 model [108 E45] (from May 1971 until November 1972)

was in	1971	1,871 units
	1972	6,302 units
	total	8,173 units

Specifications

	280SEL 4.5
Engine type	V-8 cyl overhead camshafts (M 117)
Bore and stroke	92 x 85mm (3.62 x 3.35 in)
Displacement	4520 cc (275.8 cu in)
Power output	225 hp (DIN) @ 5000 rpm (250 hp SAE) U.S.: 230 hp SAE @ 5000 rpm
Compression ratio	8.8:1 U.S.: 8:1
Torque	38.5 mkg @ 3000 rpm (278.5 ft/lb)
Fuel injection	Bosch electronic
Engine speed at 100 km/hr	2865 rpm U.S.: 2740 rpm
Gear ratios	I. 3.98:1 U.S. automatic I. 2.31:1 II. 2.39:1 II. 1.46:1 III. 1.46:1 III. 1.00:1 IV. 1.00:1
Rear axle ratio	3.69 U.S.: 3.23
Chassis	unit frame and body
Suspension	independent front and rear, with coil springs, diagonal-pivot swing axle, anti-sway bars
Brakes and area	disc, front and rear vented, servo assisted, two circuit hydraulic, 273/279mm (10.8/11.0 in)
Wheelbase	2850mm (112.2 in)
Track, front/rear	1482/1490mm (58.4/58.7 in)
Length	4780mm (188.2 in)
Width	1770mm (69.7 in)
Height	1440mm (56.7 in)
Ground clearance	175mm (6.9 in)
Tires	735 H 14 or 185 H 14
Turning circle	12.2 meters (40 ft)
Steering type and ratio	recirculating ball (4.0 turns), servo assisted
Weight	1737 kg (3821 lbs)
Maximum speed	205 km/hr (127 mph) U.S.: 190 km/hr (118 mph)
Acceleration	9.5 sec 0-100 km/hr U.S.: 12 sec 0-100 km/hr
Fuel consumption	14.5 liters, super/100 km (16 mpg)
Fuel tank capacity	82 liters (21.7 gallons)

Model 300SEL 4.5 (1971-1972)

The 300SEL 4.5 model sedan was produced at the same time the 280SE/SEL models, first in May 1971. It was natural that the larger and more powerful V-8 engine would be placed into the more luxurious of the longer wheelbase sedans, so as to allow this rather formal model to remain the very best of the top line. The sedan was greatly preferred as an official and generally chauffeur-driven automobile, whenever the prestigious 600 limousine was not desired.

The 300SEL 4.5 sedan never achieved the popularity of the 280SEL 4.5 model, of course, but sales for the first year were over 600 units, while in 1972 nearly 2,000 such cars were sold. Total sales of the 300SEL 4.5 were 2,553 units and of the 280SEL 4.5 were 8,173 units during the two years of their production life.

Prices and Production

In the United States the 300SEL 4.5 sedan sold
in September 1972 for (East coast)............$ 14,130
(West coast) ....$ 14,240

Production of the 300SEL 4.5 model [109 E45] (from May 1971 until October 1972)

was in	1971	656 units
	1972	1,897 units
total		2,553 units

Specifications

	300SEL 4.5
Engine type	V-8 cyl overhead camshafts (M 117)
Bore and stroke	92 x 85mm (3.62 x 3.35 in)
Displacement	4520 cc (275.8 cu in)
Power output	225 hp (DIN) @ 5000 rpm (250 hp SAE) U.S.: 230 hp SAE @ 5000 rpm
Compression ratio	8.8:1 U.S.: 8:1
Torque	38.5 mkg @ 3000 rpm (278.5 ft/lb)
Fuel injection	Bosch electronic
Engine speed at 100 km/hr	2865 rpm U.S.: 2740 rpm
Gear ratios	I. 3.98:1 U.S. automatic I. 2.31:1 II. 2.39:1 II. 1.46:1 III. 1.46:1 III. 1.00:1 IV. 1.00:1
Rear axle ratio	3.69 U.S.: 3.23
Chassis	unit frame and body
Suspension	independent front and rear, with coil springs, diagonal-pivot swing axle, anti-sway bars
Brakes and area	disc, front vented, rear solid, servo assisted, two circuit hydraulic, 273/279mm (10.8/11.0 in)
Wheelbase	2850mm (112.2 in)
Track, front/rear	1482/1490mm (58.4/58.7 in)
Length	4780mm (188.2 in)
Width	1770mm (69.7 in)
Height	1440mm (56.7 in)
Ground clearance	175mm (6.9 in)
Tires	735 H 14 or 185 H 14
Turning circle	12.2 meters (40 ft)
Steering type and ratio	recirculating ball (4.0 turns), servo assisted
Weight	1854 kg (4079 lbs)
Maximum speed	205 km/hr (127 mph) U.S.: 190 km/hr (118 mph)
Acceleration	9.5 sec 0-100 km/hr U.S.: 12 sec 0-100 km/hr
Fuel consumption	14.5 liters, super/100 km (16 mpg)
Fuel tank capacity	82 liters (21.7 gallons)

Model 450SL (1971-   )

The 450SL model was shown to the public at the Geneva Auto Show in 1973 but had been produced for the United States market earlier, in 1971. It was a more powerful car than the 3.5-liter version and retained all of the fine attributes of this new model sports car.

The U.S. version of the 450SL (outwardly identifiable by the different headlight arrangement only), had a lowered compression ratio to 8:1 and milder camshafts. The car was equipped with heavier bumpers and was fitted with the new three-speed automatic transmission only. Rear axle ratio was changed to 3.07 and the maximum speed was 124 miles per hour. The 4.5-liter engine actually developed less horsepower than the original 3.5-liter unit, but that was the price to pay for the more stringent emission controls prevailing here. The car weighed 148 pounds more than the European version and had, of course, not the performance of that more powerful and lighter car.

Prices and Production

The 450SL model sold in 1973 for . . . . .DM 36,630
    in 1974 for. . . . . .DM 38,300
    in 1975 for. . . . . .DM 42,215
In the United States the 450SL coupe/roadster sold
    in September 1972 for (East coast). . . . .$ 11,688
       (West coast) . . . .$ 11,800
    in March 1973 (East coast) . . . .$ 12,733
    in November 1973 (East coast) . . . .$ 15,450
    in September 1974 (with automatic transmission)
       (East coast) . . . .$ 17,056
    in October 1975 (with automatic transmission)
       (East coast) . . . .$ 19,357

Production of the 450SL model [107 E45] (from March/July 1971)
was in 1971   2,131 units
         1972   7,473 units
         1973   8,654 units
         1974   6,093 units
         1975   6,011 units

         total   30,362 units

Specifications

	450SL
Engine type	V-8 cyl overhead camshaft (M 117)
Bore and stroke	92 x 85mm (3.62 x 3.35 in)
Displacement	4520 cc (275.8 cu in)
Power output	225 hp (DIN) @ 5000 rpm (250 hp SAE) U.S.: 230 hp SAE @ 5000 rpm (200 hp DIN) later, 190 hp SAE @ 4750 rpm; 1975 California: 180 hp SAE
Compression ratio	8.8:1 U.S.: 8:1
Torque	38.5 mkg @ 3000 rpm (278.5 ft/lb) U.S.: 33.0 mkg @ 3000 rpm (238.8 ft/lb); 1975 California: 232 ft/lb
Fuel injection	Bosch electronic
Engine speed at 100 km/hr	2865 rpm U.S.: 2700 rpm
Gear ratios	I. 3.98:1 U.S. automatic I. 2.31:1 II. 2.39:1 II. 1.46:1 III. 1.46:1 III. 1.00:1 IV. 1.00:1
Rear axle ratio	3.07
Chassis	unit frame and body
Suspension	independent front and rear, double wishbones, diagonal-pivot swing axle
Brakes and area	disc, front vented, rear solid, 278/279mm (10.9/11.0 in)
Wheelbase	2460mm (96.9 in)
Track, front/rear	1452/1440mm (57.2/56.7 in)
Length	4380mm (172.4 in) U.S.: 182.3 in
Width	1790mm (70.5 in)
Height	1300mm (51.2 in)
Ground clearance	140mm (5.5 in)
Tires	205/70 VR 14
Turning circle	10.2 meters (33.5 ft)
Steering type and ratio	recirculating ball (3.0 turns); servo assisted 15.9:1
Weight	1585 kg (3487 lbs) U.S.: 1718 kg (3780 lbs)
Maximum speed	215 km/hr (133.5 mph) U.S.: 200 km/hr (124 mph)
Acceleration	8.5 sec 0-100 km/hr U.S.: 11 sec 0-100 km/hr
Fuel consumption	14.5 liters, super/100 km (16 mpg) (U.S.: no lead fuel)
Fuel tank capacity	90 liters (23.8 gallons)

Prices and Production

The 450SLC model sold in 1973 for . . . . .DM 41,015
    in 1974 for. . . . . .DM 42,860
    in 1975 for. . . . . .DM 47,265
In the United States the 450SLC coupe sold
    in September 1972 for (East coast). . . . .$ 15,094
    (West coast) . . . .$ 15,194
    in March 1973 (East coast) . . . .$ 16,498
    in November 1973 (East coast) . . . .$ 19,450
    in September 1974 (with automatic transmission)
    (East coast) . . . .$ 21,307
    in October 1975 (with automatic transmission)
    (East coast) . . . .$ 23,976

Production of the 450SLC coupe model [107 E45] (from February/July 1972)

was in	1972	700 units
	1973	5,594 units
	1974	2,961 units
	1975	2,993 units
	total	12,248 units

Model 450SLC (1972-   )

The 450SLC model was also shown at the Geneva Show in 1973. Here again, the European version of that coupe was quite differently powered than that for sale in the United States. The restrictions placed on emission and safety added weight and lessened performance because of less horsepower developed. The 4.5-liter engine actually developed 225 DIN horsepower, while the U.S. version developed 230 SAE horsepower. Considering that the German (DIN) designation means the net horsepower available and the SAE (American) horsepower is the gross measurement, one can readily see that the heavier car with less power suffered greatly in comparison.

Outwardly there was no difference in the 350SLC or the 450SLC cars. Unlike the SL model, the coupe never was designated as the 350 4.5.

Specifications

	450SLC
Engine type	V-8 cyl overhead camshafts (M 117)
Bore and stroke	92 x 85mm (3.62 x 3.35 in)
Displacement	4520 cc (275.8 cu in)
Power output	225 hp (DIN) @ 5000 rpm (250 hp SAE) U.S.: 230 hp SAE @ 5000 rpm later, 190 hp SAE @ 4750 rpm; 1975 California: 180 hp SAE
Compression ratio	8.8:1 U.S. 8:1
Torque	38.5 mkg @ 3000 rpm (278.5 ft/lb) U.S.: 33.0 mkg @ 3000 rpm (238.8 ft/lb); 1975 California: 232 ft/lb
Fuel injection	Bosch electronic
Engine speed at 100 km/hr	2865 rpm U.S.: 2700 rpm
Gear ratios	I. 3.98:1 U.S. automatic I. 2.31:1 II. 2.39:1 II. 1.46:1 III. 1.46:1 III. 1.00:1 IV. 1.00:1
Rear axle ratio	3.07
Chassis	unit frame and body
Suspension	independent front and rear, double wishbones, diagonal-pivot swing axle
Brakes and area	disc, front vented, rear solid, 278/279mm (10.9/11.0 in)
Wheelbase	2815mm (110.8 in)
Track, front/rear	1452/1440mm (57.2/56.7 in)
Length	4740mm (186.6 in) U.S.: 196.4 in
Width	1790mm (70.5 in)
Height	1330mm (51.2 in)
Ground clearance	140mm (5.5 in)
Tires	205/70 VR 14
Turning circle	11.2 meters (36.7 ft)
Steering type and ratio	recirculating ball (3.0 turns); servo assisted 15.9:1
Weight	1635 kg (3597 lbs) U.S.: 1735 kg (3817 lbs)
Maximum speed	215 km/hr (133.5 mph) U.S.: 200 km/hr (124 mph)
Acceleration	8.5 sec 0-100 km/hr U.S.: 11 sec 0-100 km/hr
Fuel consumption	14.5 liters, super/100 km (16 mpg) (U.S. no lead fuel)
Fuel tank capacity	90 liters (23.8 gallons)

Model 280S (1972-   )

The 280S model, one of the newly designed cars of the S-class, was first shown at the Paris Automobile Salon in 1972. It was the least expensive representative of the almost completely restyled new line of the large six- and eight-cylinder models which shared the same basic chassis and body.

The car appeared slightly wider, lower, and longer than the previous ones. The radiator shell was longer and wider and the front light section was integrated into a wide unit curving around to the side. The rear light cluster was also redesigned in the manner of the sports models, with the dirt-repelling feature. Many new safety features had been incorporated into the design.

The modified chassis had the new suspension system of the SL and SLC models which had proved superior to the former design.

The double overhead camshaft six-cylinder engine developed 160 DIN horsepower, but for the United States a detuned version of 120 SAE horsepower was supplied, with lowered compression ratio, for improved emission. It had a torque converter four-speed automatic transmission. That car also weighed 350 pounds more than the European model, and had consequently less performance. Still, the maximum speed was 170 kilometers (105 miles) per hour.

Prices and Production

The 280S four-door sedan sold in 1972 for. . . . . .DM 23,810
   in 1973 for. . . . . .DM 25,030
   in 1974 for. . . . . .DM 26,165
   in 1975 for. . . . . .DM 28,050
In the United States the 280S sedan sold
   in September 1974 for (fully equipped)
     (East coast) . . . .$ 14,548
     (West coast) . . . .$ 14,698
   in October 1975 (East coast). . . . .$ 16,545

Production of the 280S model [116 V28] (from August/September 1972)

	was in	1972	3,787 units
		1973	15,340 units
		1974	20,808 units
		1975	21,996 units
		total	61,931 units

Specifications

	280S
Engine type	6 cyl double overhead camshafts (M110)
Bore and stroke	86 x 78.8mm (3.41 x 3.10 in)
Displacement	2746 cc (168 cu in)
Power output	160 hp (DIN) @ 5500 rpm (180 hp SAE) U. S.: 120 hp SAE @ 4800 rpm; 1975 California: 123 hp SAE @ 5000 rpm
Compression ratio	9:1 U.S. 8:1
Torque	23 mkg @ 4000 rpm (166.4 ft/lb) U.S.: 15.5 mkg @ 2800 rpm (112.1 ft/lb) 1975: 143 ft/lb @ 2800 rpm; California: 143 @ 3600 rpm
Carburetion	dual downdraft carburetor Solex 4 A 1
Engine speed at 100 km/hr	3140 rpm
Gear ratios	I. 3.98:1 (14.69) II. 2.39:1 (8.82) III. 1.46:1 (5.39) IV. 1.00:1 (3.69)
Rear axle ratio	3.69
Chassis	unit frame and body
Suspension	independent front and rear, double wishbones, diagonal-pivot swing axle
Brakes and area	disc, front vented, rear solid, 278/279mm (10.9/11.0)
Wheelbase	2865mm (112.8 in)
Track, front/rear	1525/1505mm (60.0/59.3 in)
Length	4960mm (195.3 in)
Width	1865mm (73.4 in)
Height	1425mm (56.1 in)
Ground clearance	150mm (5.9 in)
Tires	185 HR 14
Turning circle	11.4 meters (37.4 ft)
Steering type and ratio	recirculating ball (2.7 turns); servo assisted 15.6:1
Weight	1610 kg (3542 lbs) U.S.: 3890 lbs
Maximum speed	190 km/hr (118 mph) U.S.: 170 km/hr (105.5 mph)
Acceleration	13.5 sec 0-100 km/hr; (U.S.: no lead fuel)
Fuel consumption	12.5 liters/100 km (18.75 mpg)
Fuel tank capacity	96 liters (25.4 gallons)

Model 280SE (1972-   )

The 280SE model, also introduced at the Paris Salon in 1972, was the fuel-injected version of the six-cylinder sedan of the newly designed S-class of passenger cars. It had the same dimensions as the carburetor model and shared the body and chassis with the more powerful eight-cylinder cars.

The new model weighed 124 kilograms (273 pounds) more than the former 280SE model which it replaced, but with the double overhead camshaft engine of 185 DIN horsepower, against the 160 formerly, the performance was actually superior to the older model.

Prices and Production

The 280SE four-door sedan sold in 1972 for . . . . .DM 25,530
   in 1973 for. . . . . .DM 26,810
   in 1974 for. . . . . .DM 28,020
   in 1975 for. . . . . .DM 30,900

Production of the 280SE model [116 E28] (from August/September 1972)

	was in	1972	3,737 units
		1973	18,266 units
		1974	18,634 units
		1975	17,376 units
		total	58,013 units

Specifications

	280SE
Engine type	6 cyl double overhead camshafts (M 110)
Bore and stroke	86 x 78.8mm (3.41 x 3.10 in)
Displacement	2746 cc (168 cu in)
Power output	185 hp (DIN) @ 6000 rpm (205 hp SAE)
Compression ratio	9:1
Torque	24.5 mkg @ 4500 rpm (175.8 ft/lb)
Fuel injection	Bosch electronic
Engine speed at 100 km/hr	3140 rpm
Gear ratios	I. 3.98:1 (14.69) II. 2.39:1 (8.82) III. 1.46:1 (5.39) IV. 1.00:1 (3.69)
Rear axle ratio	3.69
Chassis	unit frame and body
Suspension	independent front and rear, double wishbones, diagonal-pivot swing axle
Brakes and area	disc, front vented, rear solid, 278/279mm (10.9/11.0 in)
Wheelbase	2865mm (112.8 in)
Track, front/rear	1525/1505mm (60.0/59.3 in)
Length	4960mm (195.3 in)
Width	1865mm (73.4 in)
Height	1425mm (56.1 in)
Ground clearance	150mm (5.9 in)
Tires	185 HR 14
Turning circle	11.4 meters (37.4 ft)
Steering type and ratio	recirculating ball (2.7 turns); servo assisted 15.6:1
Weight	1610 kg (3542 lbs)
Maximum speed	200 km/hr (124 mph)
Acceleration	12.5 sec 0-100 km/hr
Fuel consumption	12.5 liters/100 km (18.75 mpg)
Fuel tank capacity	96 liters (25.4 gallons)

Model 350SE (1972-   )

The 350SE was the third of the newly designed cars of the S-class which made their debut at the Paris Auto Show in 1972. It was the eight-cylinder edition of this new body style automobile. With the 3.5-liter displacement engine of 200 DIN horsepower and a weight of 1,675 kilograms (3,685 pounds), the car achieved a maximum speed of 205 kilometers (127 miles) per hour and accelerated to 100 kilometers in 11.5 seconds, a fine performance figure. (Torque was rated at 32 mkg or 321 ft/lb. at 4,200 rpm.)

That these newly styled and improved cars were well accepted by the automobile-buying public is indicated by the production figures. For 1972 it was about 4,000 units (of each of the three new models) and for the first full year of manufacture it reached nearly 15,000 units.

Prices and Production

The 350SE four-door sedan sold in 1972 for. . . . . . . .DM 28,860
   in 1973 for. . . . . .DM 30,260
   in 1974 for. . . . . .DM 31,615
   in 1975 for. . . . . .DM 34,860

Production of the 350SE model [116 E35] (from March/August 1972)

was in	1972	4,353 units
	1973	14,340 units
	1974	7,266 units
	1975	5,447 units
	total	31,406 units

Specifications

	350SE
Engine type	V-8 cyl overhead camshafts (M 116)
Bore and stroke	92 x 65.8mm (3.62 x 2.59 in)
Displacement	3499 cc (213.5 cu in)
Power output	200 hp (DIN) @ 5800 rpm (230 hp SAE @ 6050 rpm)
Compression ratio	9.5:1
Torque	29.2 mkg @ 4000 rpm (32 mkg @ 4200 rpm 231.5 ft/lb)
Fuel injection	Bosch electronic
Engine speed at 100 km/hr	2945 rpm
Gear ratios	I. 3.90:1 II. 2.30:1 III. 1.41:1 IV. 1.00:1
Rear axle ratio	3.46
Chassis	unit frame and body
Suspension	independent front and rear, double wishbones, diagonal-pivot swing axle
Brakes and area	disc, front vented, rear solid, 278/279mm (10.9/11.0 in)
Wheelbase	2865mm (112.8 in)
Track, front/rear	1525/1505mm (60.0/59.3 in)
Length	4960mm (195.3 in)
Width	1865mm (73.4 in)
Height	1425mm (56.1 in)
Ground clearance	150mm (5.9 in)
Tires	205/70 HR 14
Turning circle	11.4 meters (37.4 ft)
Steering type and ratio	recirculating ball (2.7 turns); servo assisted 15.6:1
Weight	1675 kg (3685 lbs)
Maximum speed	205 km/hr (127 mph)
Acceleration	11.5 sec 0-100 km/hr
Fuel consumption	13 liters/100 km (18 mpg)
Fuel tank capacity	96 liters (25.4 gallons)

Model 230/4 (1972-1975)

The 230/4 model was one of the two new passenger car models first introduced at the Frankfurt Auto Show in 1973. It replaced the 220 sedan which had been manufactured since 1967. The new four-cylinder engine with a stroke of 83.6 milimeters and bore of 93.75 millimeters developed 110 horsepower and gave the sedan a maximum speed of 170 kilometers (106 miles) per hour against the 161 of the former. Acceleration was the same. However, the new engine used less effort to accomplish this.

The new body had a wider radiator grille and was slightly lower in front and was similar to those of the current S-class models. With these eleven larger models the four-cylinder car shared the suspension and other, modern advanced design and safety features. A total of twenty-four different models of passenger cars were offered that year.

Prices and Production

The 230/4 four-door sedan sold in 1973 for . . . . .DM 15,210
   in 1974 for. . . . . .DM 15,875
   in 1975 for. . . . . .DM 17,505
   Power steering . . . . .DM   515
   Automatic transmission .DM 1,440
In the United States the 230 sedan sold
   in November 1973 for (with automatic transmission)
      (East coast) . . . .$ 8,420
      (West coast) . . . .$ 8,530
   in September 1974 (East coast) . . . .$ 9,357
   in October 1975 (East coast). . . . .$ 10,497

Production of the 230/4 model [115 V23] (from January/August 1973)

	was in	1972	7 units
		1973	9,568 units
		1974	30,013 units
		1975	35,073 units
		total	74,661 units

Specifications

	230/4
Engine type	4 cyl overhead camshaft (M 115)
Bore and stroke	93.75 x 83.6mm (3.69 x 3.29 in)
Displacement	2277 cc (140.8 cu in)
Power output	110 hp (DIN) @ 4800 rpm; (U.S.: 95 hp SAE @ 4800 rpm) 1975: 93 hp SAE @ 4800 rpm 1975 California: 85 hp SAE @ 4500 rpm
Compression ratio	9:1 U.S. 8:1
Torque	19 mkg @ 2500 rpm (137.5 ft/lb); U.S.: 17.7 mkg @ 2500 rpm 128 ft/lb 1975: 125 ft/lb, California: 122 ft/lb
Carburetion	Crossdraft carburetor Stromberg 175 CDT
Engine speed at 100 km/hr	3180 rpm
Gear ratios	I. 3.90:1 II. 2.30:1 III. 1.41:1 IV. 1.00:1
Rear axle ratio	3.69 U.S. 3.92
Chassis	unit frame and body
Suspension	independent front and rear, double wishbones, diagonal-pivot swing axle, anti- sway bars
Brakes and area	disc, hydraulic dual circuit, 273/279mm (10.8/11.0 in)
Wheelbase	2750mm (108.3 in)
Track, front/rear	1448/1.440mm (57.0/56.7 in)
Length	4680mm (184.3 in) U.S.: 195.5 in
Width	1770mm (69.7 in)
Height	1440mm (56.7 in)
Ground clearance	175mm (6.9 in)
Tires	175 SR 14
Turning circle	11 meters (36.1 ft)
Steering type and ratio	recirculating ball(3.0 turns), servo assisted
Weight	1350 kg (2970 lbs) U.S.: 1470 kg (3234 lbs)
Maximum speed	170 km/hr (106 mph)
Acceleration	13.7 sec 0-100 km/hr
Fuel consumption	11.4 liters, super/100 km (20.5 mpg) (U.S.: no lead fuel)
Fuel tank capacity	65 liters (17.2 gallons)

Model 240D (1973-)

The 240D sedan was one of two new models first shown to the public at the Frankfurt Auto Show in 1973. It was an addition to the fast-selling diesel-engined passenger cars of the 200D and 220D models. With a larger displacement, the four-cylinder engine developed 65 horsepower (against the 55 and 60 of the other two models). It shared with the new 230.4 engine other advancements in engine design.

In the customary tradition, the body style of these two cars was exactly alike. All of the new features of the gasoline-engined model were available to those who preferred the fantastic economy of the diesel-engined car. With the cylinder dimensions of the 240D, engineers believed that they had achieved the ultimate in passenger car development, for the 600 cubic centimeter displacement seemed the very ideal size.

The 240D engine ran slower than the others (at 3,180 revolutions against 3,375 at 100 kilometers per hour) and maximum speed was increased to 138 kilometers per hour against the 130 and 135 of the smaller engined cars.

In August 1973 the long chassis diesel limousine had the 240D engine installed instead of the former 220D. All of the specifications of the earlier model applied to this one except for the maximum speed (now 135 km/hr; automatic: 130 km/hr.) and the fuel consumption (now 11.5 liters; automatic: 12.5 liters per 100 kilometers). The overall weight had also increased slightly (by 15 kg) to 1,555 kg (3,421 lbs.).

Prices and Production

The 240D four-door sedan sold in 1973 for . . . . .DM 15,985
    in 1974 for. . . . . .DM 16,710
    in 1975 for. . . . . .DM 18,425
    Power steering . . . . .DM   515
    Automatic transmission . . . . .DM 1,440
The 240D long-wheelbase limousine sold in 1973 for . . .DM 22,590
    but the price increased gradually until it reached
        in 1975 . . . . .DM 26,075
In the United States the 240D sedan sold
    in November 1973 for (East coast) . . . .$ 8,140
    (West coast) . . . .$ 8,250
    and with automatic transmission (East coast) . . . . . .$ 8,715
    (West coast) . . . .$ 8,825
    in September 1974 (East coast) . . . .$ 8,862
        and with automatic transmission . . . .$ 9,479
    in October 1975 (East coast) . . . .$ 9,930
        and with automatic transmission . . . .$ 10,621

Production of the 240D model [115 D24] (from February/August 1973)

was in	1973	16,512 units
	1974	60,928 units
	1975	38,019 units
	total	115,459 units

Specifications

	240D
Engine type	4 cyl overhead camshaft (OM 616)
Bore and stroke	91 x 92.4mm (3.58 x 3.64 in)
Displacement	2376 cc (146.7 cu in)
Power output	65 hp (DIN) @ 4200 rpm (62 hp SAE @ 4000 rpm)
Compression ratio	21:1
Torque	14 mkg @ 2400 rpm (13.4 mkg 97 ft/lb @ 2400 rpm)
Fuel injection	Bosch four plunger pump
Engine speed at 100 km/hr	3180 rpm
Gear ratios	I. 3.90:1 II. 2.30:1 III. 1.41:1 IV. 1.00:1
Rear axle ratio	3.69
Chassis	unit frame and body
Suspension	independent front and rear, double wishbones, diagonal-pivot swing axle, anti- sway bars
Brakes and area	disc, hydraulic dual circuit, 273/279mm (10.8/11.0 in)
Wheelbase	2750mm (108.3 in)
Track, front/rear	1448/1440mm (57.0/56.7 in)
Length	4680mm (184.3 in) U.S.: 195.5 in
Width	1770mm (69.7 in)
Height	1440mm (56.7 in)
Ground clearance	175mm (6.9 in)
Tires	175 SR 14
Turning circle	11 meters (36.1 ft)
Steering type and ratio	recirculating ball (3.0 turns), servo assisted
Weight	1390 kg (3058 lbs) U.S.: 1457 kg (3205 lbs)
Maximum speed	138 km/hr (85.7 mph)
Acceleration	24.6 sec 0-100 km/hr
Fuel consumption	9.5 liters/100 km (24.75 mpg)
Fuel tank capacity	65 liters (17.2 gallons) 1976: 80 liters (20.6 gallons)

Model 280SEL (1973-   )

The 280SEL was first shown at the Geneva Salon in early 1974. In the true tradition of the company, it was a stretched version of the 280SE model sedan. The wheelbase was, as before on these long models, ten centimeters longer than that of the regular sedan, all of which benefitted the passengers in the rear seat. With the same engine of 2.8 liters displacement and 185 horsepower (DIN), the performance was equal to that of the shorter car. Maximum speed was calculated at 200 kilometers (124 miles) per hour.

The 280SEL model was one of twenty-four different passenger car models offered that year by Mercedes-Benz and fulfilled the specific needs of a wide range of preference by the motorists.

Prices and Production

The 280SEL four-door sedan sold in 1974 for. . . . . . . .DM 30,680
  in 1975 for. . . . . .DM 33,340

Production of the 280SEL model [116 E28] (from October 1973/April 1974)

was in	1973	1 unit
	1974	535 units
	1975	716 units
	total	1,252 units

Specifications

	280SEL
Engine type	6 cyl double overhead camshafts (M 110)
Bore and stroke	86 x 78.8mm (3.41 x 3.10 in)
Displacement	2746 cc (168 cu in)
Power output	185 hp (DIN) @ 6000 rpm (205 hp SAE)
Compression ratio	9:1
Torque	24.3 mkg @ 4500 rpm (175.8 ft/lb)
Fuel injection	Bosch electronic
Engine speed at 100 km/hr	3140 rpm
Gear ratios	I. 3.90:1 II. 2.30:1 III. 1.41:1 IV. 1.00:1
Rear axle ratio	3.69
Chassis	unit frame and body
Suspension	independent front and rear, double wishbones, diagonal-pivot swing axle, anti-sway bars
Brakes and area	disc, power assisted, two circuit hydraulic, 278/279mm (10.9/11.0 in)
Wheelbase	2965mm (116.7 in)
Track, front/rear	1525/1505mm (60/59.3 in)
Length	5060mm (199.2 in)
Width	1865mm (73.4 in)
Height	1430mm (56.3 in)
Ground clearance	147mm (5.8 in)
Tires	185 HR 14
Turning circle	11.9 meters (39 ft)
Steering type and ratio	recirculating ball (3.0 turns), servo assisted
Weight	1645 kg (3619 lbs)
Maximum speed	200 km/hr (124 mph)
Acceleration	12 sec 0-100 km/hr
Fuel consumption	12.5 liters/100 km (18.75 mpg)
Fuel tank capacity	96 liters (25.4 gallons)

Model 350SEL (1973-   )

The 350SEL was the other of the two new models shown first to the public at the Geneva Auto Show in 1974. It was, if anything, a more luxurious version of the other longer wheelbase sedan exhibited at the Salon. With the 3.5-liter eight-cylinder engine, identical to that of the 350SE model, developing 200 (DIN) horsepower, it had a slightly better maximum speed (205 kilometers per hour) than that of the six-cylinder 280SEL model.

With other models of the S-class, the new 350SEL sedan shared all of the newest safety and technical features of this top line of cars.

Prices and Production

The 350SEL four-door sedan sold in 1973 for. . . . . . . .DM 34,865
   in 1974 for. . . . . .DM 36,415
   in 1975 for. . . . . .DM 40,160

Production of the 350SEL model [116 E35] (from September/November 1973)

was in	1973	58 units
	1974	529 units
	1975	552 units
	total	1,139 units

Specifications

	350SEL
Engine type	V-8 cyl overhead camshafts (M 116)
Bore and stroke	92 x 65.8mm (3.62 x 2.59 in)
Displacement	3499 cc (213.5 cu in)
Power output	200 hp (DIN) @ 5800 rpm (230 hp SAE @ 6050 rpm)
Compression ratio	9.5:1
Torque	29.2 mkg @ 4000 rpm (32 mkg @ 4200 rpm 231.5 ft/lb)
Fuel injection	Bosch electronic
Engine speed at 100 km/hr	2945 rpm
Gear ratios	I. 3.90:1 II. 2.30:1 III. 1.41:1 IV. 1.00:1
Rear axle ratio	3.46
Chassis	unit frame and body
Suspension	independent front and rear, double wishbones, diagonal-pivot swing axle, anti-sway bars
Brakes and area	disc, power assisted, two circuit hydraulic, 278/279mm (10.9/11.0 in)
Wheelbase	2965mm (116.7 in)
Track, front/rear	1525/1505mm (60/59.3 in)
Length	5060mm (199.2 in)
Width	1865mm (73.4 in)
Height	1430mm (56.3 in)
Ground clearance	147mm (5.8 in)
Tires	205/70 HR 14
Turning circle	11.9 meters (39 ft)
Steering type and ratio	recirculating ball (3.0 turns), servo assisted
Weight	1700 kg (3740 lbs)
Maximum speed	205 km/hr (127 mph)
Acceleration	11.5 sec 0-100 km/hr
Fuel consumption	13 liters/100 km (18 mpg)
Fuel tank capacity	96 liters (25.4 gallons)

Model 450SE (1972-)

The 450SE sedan was introduced to the public at the Geneva Salon in March 1973. Along with the 450SEL, 450SLC, these cars represented the top of the S-class and included all of the newest technological and safety features developed by the engineers. These incorporated design features of the C111 experimental car, such as the front axle geometry and design first tested on that amazing vehicle, and increased lateral and roll-over protection, distinct crumble zones and other safety features first tested with the experimental safety vehicles ESF 5, 13 and 22.

The 450SE was quickly recognized as one of the finest cars ever produced by Daimler-Benz and the group of forty-five European automotive journalists voted it the Car of the Year. The basic criteria were overall engineering concept with special regard to safety, aesthetic impression, styling and design, and price in relation to value offered.

While the 450SE had the 225 horsepower (DIN) engine and three- or four-speed torque converter, the U.S. version had a detuned unit which developed 190 SAE horsepower and had the three-speed automatic transmission only. Still, *Road & Track* considered the car the Best Sedan in the World.

In Europe the car was also judged Car of the Year by the automotive journalists representing six leading publications: Auto Visie of Holland, Stern of Germany, Daily Telegraph Magazine of Britain, L'Equipe of France, Quattroruote of Italy and ViBilägare of Sweden.

Prices and Production

The 450SE four-door sedan sold in 1973 for	.DM	33,970
in 1974 for	.DM	35,500
in 1975 for	.DM	39,150

The 450SE four-door sedan sold in the United States
in March 1973 for (fully equipped)

(East coast)	.$	13,396
(West coast)	.$	13,491
in November 1973 (East coast)	.$	15,820
in September 1974 (East coast)	.$	17,713
in October 1975 (East coast)	.$	19,989

Production of the 450SE model [116 E45] (from August/December 1972)

was in	1972	52 units
	1973	13,400 units
	1974	7,579 units
	1975	4,672 units
	total	25,703 units

Specifications

	450SE
Engine type	V-8 cyl overhead camshafts (M 117)
Bore and stroke	92 x 85mm (3.62 x 3.35 in)
Displacement	4520 cc (275.8 cu in)
Power output	225 hp (DIN) @ 5000 rpm; U.S.: 190 hp SAE @ 4750 rpm 1975 California: 180 hp SAE
Compression ratio	8.8:1 U.S.: 8:1
Torque	38.5 mkg @ 3000 rpm (278.5 ft/lb) U.S.: 33.0 mkg @ 3000 rpm (238.8 ft/lb); 1975 California: 232 ft/lb
Fuel injection	Bosch electronic
Engine speed at 100 km/hr	2865 rpm U.S.: 2700 rpm
Gear ratios	I. 3.98:1 U.S. automatic I. 2.31:1 II. 2.39:1 II. 1.46:1 III. 1.46:1 III. 1.00:1 IV. 1.00:1
Rear axle ratio	3.07
Chassis	unit frame and body
Suspension	independent front and rear, double wishbones, diagonal-pivot swing axle
Brakes and area	disc, front vented, rear solid, 278/279mm (10.9/11.0 in)
Wheelbase	2860mm (112.6 in)
Track, front/rear	1525/1505mm (60.0/59.3 in)
Length	4960mm (195.3 in) U.S.: 205.5 in
Width	1870mm (73.6 in)
Height	1425mm (56.1 in)
Ground clearance	150mm (5.9 in)
Tires	205/70 VR 14
Turning circle	11.4 meters (37.4 ft)
Steering type and ratio	recirculating ball (2.7 turns); servo assisted 15.6:1
Weight	1740 kg (3828 lbs) U.S.: 4070 lbs
Maximum speed	210 km/hr (130 mph) U.S.: 205 km/hr (127 mph)
Acceleration	9.3 sec 0-100 km/hr U.S.: 10.8 sec 0-100 km/hr
Fuel consumption	14.5 liters/100 km (16 mpg) (U.S.: no lead fuel)
Fuel tank capacity	96 liters (25.4 gallons)

Model 450SEL (1972-   )

The 450SEL sedan, also first shown at the Geneva Auto Show in 1973, was basically the same car as the regular length 450SE. With a ten-centimeter longer wheelbase, only the rear passenger benefited from that change. The interior was exactly the same as that of the SE model, with headrest, safety belts, electrically operated windows, center locking system, and such safety features as standard equipment.

The rear diagonal swing axle had been further developed for the 450 models because of the high torque and fitted with an anti-squat device, eliminating entirely rear end dipping when aggressively accelerating from a standstill. The hydraulic dual circuit brake with vacuum booster and disc brakes on all four wheels was, of course, standard on these models as on the other S-class cars.

In the United States, the 450SEL had the same detuned engine as the regular sedan and shared all other alterations with it to comply with the more stringent emission controls and regulations on safety.

Prices and Production

The 450SEL four-door sedan sold in 1973 for . . . . . . .DM 38,575
    in 1974 for. . . . . .DM 40,300
    in 1975 for. . . . . .DM 44,450
The 450SEL four-door sedan sold in the United States
    in March 1973 for (fully equipped)
        (East coast) . . . .$ 14,605
        (West coast) . . . .$ 14,698
    in November 1973 (East coast) . . . .$ 17,400
    in September 1974 (East coast) . . . .$ 19,106
    in October 1975 (East coast) . . . .$ 21,709

Production of the 450SEL model [116 E45] (from December 1972)
            was in 1972   24 units
                  1973 6,930 units
                  1974 8,350 units
                  1975 6,167 units
                                  ——————
                 total 21,471 units

Specifications

	450SEL
Engine type	V-8 cyl overhead camshafts (M 117)
Bore and stroke	92 x 85mm (3.62 x 3.35 in)
Displacement	4520 cc (275.8 cu in)
Power output	225 hp (DIN) @ 5000 rpm U.S.: 190 hp SAE @ 4750 rpm; 1975 California: 180 hp SAE
Compression ratio	8.8:1 U.S. 8:1
Torque	38.5 mkg @ 3000 rpm (278.5 ft/lb) U.S.: 33.0 mkg @ 3000 rpm (240 ft/lb); 1975 California: 232 ft/lb
Fuel injection	Bosch electronic
Engine speed at 100 km/hr	2865 rpm U.S.: 2700 rpm
Gear ratios	I. 3.98:1 U.S. automatic I. 2.31:1 II. 2.39:1 II. 1.46:1 III. 1.46:1 III. 1.00:1 IV. 1.00:1
Rear axle ratio	3.07
Chassis	unit frame and body
Suspension	independent front and rear, double wishbones, diagonal-pivot swing axle
Brakes and area	disc, front vented, rear solid, 278/279mm (10.9/11.0 in)
Wheelbase	2960mm (116.5 in)
Track, front/rear	1525/1505mm (60.0/59.3 in)
Length	5060mm (199.2 in) U.S.: 209.4 in
Width	1870mm (73.6 in)
Height	1430mm (56.3 in)
Ground clearance	150mm (5.9 in)
Tires	205/70 VR 14
Turning circle	11.8 meters (38.4 ft)
Steering type and ratio	recirculating ball (2.7 turns); servo assisted 15.6:1
Weight	1740 kg (3828 lbs) U.S.: 4100 lbs
Maximum speed	210 km/hr (130 mph) U.S.: 205 km/hr (127 mph)
Acceleration	9.3 sec 0-100 km/hr U.S.: 10.8 sec 0-100 km/hr
Fuel consumption	14.5 liters/100 km (16 mpg) (U.S.: no lead fuel)
Fuel tank capacity	96 liters (25.4 gallons)

Model 230/6 (1973-   )

The 230/6 model made its appearance in late 1973 when the fuel crisis became a matter of serious concern to motorists and manufacturers in Europe. Utilizing the same body style as that of the other ten cars in the medium price range of the S-class models, the small six-cylinder engine was placed into it to create a lower priced as well as lower fuel consumption car than the regular 2.8-liter models.

A five-speed transmission was available on request in this model as on the 250, 280, and the three coupe styles. A fifth gear was designed as a high speed gear or overdrive. It lowered the engine speed and reduced fuel consumption, engine noise, and wear. The automatic torque converter four-speed transmission, as used on the 2.8-liter models, could also be fitted.

The 230.6 model was superior in performance to the four-cylinder model which it closely resembled. The car offered the flexibility of a six-cylinder engine and even greater fuel economy than the four-cylinder model at a considerably lower price than the regular sixes.

Prices and Production

The 230/6 four-door sedan sold in 1973 for . . . . .DM 16,765
    in 1974 for. . . . . .DM 17,485
    in 1975 for . . . . .DM 19,270
The 230/6 long four-door sedan sold in 1973 for. . . . .DM 23,145
    in 1974 for. . . . . .DM 24,200
    in 1975 for. . . . . .DM 26,685
Power steering . . . . .DM   515
Automatic transmission .DM 1,440

Production (figures included in the previously described 230 sedan)
[114 V23]

	was in	1973	31,378 units
		1974	25,314 units
		1975	22,992 units
		total	79,684 units

Specifications

	230/6
Engine type	6 cyl overhead camshaft (M 180)
Bore and stroke	81.75 x 72.8mm (3.23 x 2.87 in)
Displacement	2292 cc (139.9 cu in)
Power output	120 hp (DIN) @ 5400 rpm
Compression ratio	9:1
Torque	18.2 mkg @ 3600 rpm (131.7 ft/lb)
Carburetion	dual downdraft carburetor Zenith 35/40 INAT
Engine speed at 100 km/hr	3180 rpm
Gear ratios	I. 3.90:1 II. 2.30:1 III. 1.41:1 IV. 1.00:1
Rear axle ratio	3.69 (for 5-speed 3.92)
Chassis	unit frame and body
Suspension	independent front and rear, double wishbones, diagonal-pivot swing axle, anti-sway bars
Brakes and area	disc, hydraulic dual circuit, 273/279mm (10.8/11.0 in)
Wheelbase	2750mm (108.3 in)
Track, front/rear	1448/1440mm (57.0/56.7 in)
Length	4680mm (184.3 in)
Width	1770mm (69.7 in)
Height	1440mm (56.7 in)
Ground clearance	175mm (6.9 in)
Tires	175 SR 14
Turning circle	11 meters (36.1 ft)
Steering type and ratio	recirculating ball (3.0 turns), servo assisted
Weight	1365 kg (3003 lbs)
Maximum speed	175 km/hr (109 mph)
Acceleration	13.5 sec 0-100 km/hr
Fuel consumption	11.2 liters/100 km (21.5 mpg)
Fuel tank capacity	65 liters (17.2 gallons)

Model 240D 3.0/300D (1974-)

The 240D 3.0 made its appearance in July 1974. It was a radical and startling solution to the problem of increasing the available horsepower in a diesel-engined car and still maintain its size. Designated as the 300D in the United States, it was a luxury sedan of the S-class and was priced only slightly under that of the 280 sedan ($11,782 against $12,325), fully equipped with radio, air conditioning, power steering, power brakes, et al.

The five-cylinder diesel engine was basically the same as the four-cylinder unit of the 240D, except that another cylinder had been added. All dimensions and essential construction features were alike, but the Bosch injection pump was entirely redesigned. A centrifugal governor operated the metering rack and regulated the power output. The starting of the cold engine was decidedly easier than on previous diesel models, taking but a short time for the glow plug to heat up. Cylinder crank head and housing, head gasket, and the six main bearing crankshaft and oil pan were also new. Developing 80 DIN horsepower (U.S.: 77 SAE) and 17.5 mkg (U.S.: 115 ft/lb.) of torque, it gave the amazingly economical sedan a maximum speed of 92 miles (148 kilometers) per hour with the 3.46:1 rear axle ratio. The 240D, with the 3.69:1 rear axle ratio, had a maximum speed of 85.7 miles (138 kilometers) per hour.

Prices and Production

The 240D 3.0 four-door sedan sold in 1974 for . . . . . . .DM 18,815
   in 1975 for. . . . . .DM 19,915
In the United States the 300D sedan sold
   in September 1974 for (fully equipped)
      (East coast) . . . .$ 11,782
      (West coast) . . . .$ 11,921
   in October 1975 (East coast) . . . .$ 13,582

Production of the 240D 3.0 four-door sedan [115 D30] (from May 1974)

was in	1974	7,650 units
	1975	34,420 units
	total	42,070 units

Specifications

240D 3.0 / (300D)

Engine type	5 cyl overhead camshaft (OM 617)
Bore and stroke	91 x 92.4mm (3.58 x 3.64 in)
Displacement	2971 cc (183.4 cu in)
Power output	80 hp (DIN) @ 4000 rpm (77 hp SAE @ 4000 rpm)
Compression ratio	21:1
Torque	17.5 mkg @ 2400 rpm (16 mkg @ 2400 rpm 115.7 ft/lb)
Fuel injection	Bosch injector pump
Engine speed at 100 km/hr	2980 rpm
Gear ratios	I. 3.98:1 (13.77)
	II. 2.39:1 (8.27)
	III. 1.46:1 (5.05)
	IV. 1.00:1 (3.46)
Rear axle ratio	3.46
Chassis	unit frame and body
Suspension	independent front and rear, double wishbones, diagonal-pivot swing axle
Brakes and area	disc, front vented, rear solid, 273/279mm (10.8/11.0 in)
Wheelbase	2750mm (108.3 in)
Track, front/rear	1448/1440mm (57.0/56.7 in)
Length	4680mm (184.3 in) U.S.: 195.5 in
Width	1770mm (69.7 in)
Height	1440mm (56.7 in)
Ground clearance	175mm (6.9 in)
Tires	175 SR 14
Turning circle	11 meters (36.1 ft)
Steering type and ratio	recirculating ball (3.0 turns), servo assisted
Weight	1430 kg (3146 lbs) U.S.: 3450 lbs
Maximum speed	148 km/hr (92 mph) U.S.: 89 mph (143 km/hr)
Acceleration	20.6 sec 0-100 km/hr
Fuel consumption	10.8 liters/100 km (21.5 mpg)
Fuel tank capacity	65 liters (17.2 gallons); 1976: 80 liters (20.6 gallons)

Cutaway view of the 3-liter diesel engine (OM 617) and the unique 5-cylinder arrangement.

149

Prices and Production

The 450SEL 6.9 four-door sedan sold in 1975 for . . . . .DM 70,000

Production of the 450SEL 6.9 four-door sedan [116 E69] (from February/September 1975)

was in 1975   474 units

Model 450SEL 6.9 (1975-   )

The 450SEL 6.9 model was first publicly shown in 1974. It was a fast, powerful luxury sedan in the manner of the 300SEL 6.3 of 1968-1972. The sedan utilized the same body and chassis of the larger S-class, but had a hydropneumatic suspension system with four spring units carrying the weight of the vehicle. A constant self-leveling device kept the car at an even level under all road or load conditions, giving it a superb roadability. All of the technological improvements of the time were incorporated in the construction, making it truly an excellent automobile in every respect.

The 6.9-liter V-8 engine was an enlarged version of the tested powerplant used so successfully in the former 6.3 model and currently in the large 600 models. Many improvements had been accomplished since the time it was first introduced in the 6.3 sedan. With greater torque (405 ft/lb. against 369) and an increase in actual DIN horsepower to 286 from 250 formerly, the new 450SEL 6.9 car had a maximum speed of 140 miles (225 kilometers) per hour, although the new car weighed about 400 pounds more than the 6.3 model. The final drive had been reduced to 2.65:1 (against 2.85:1) which gave it a slightly greater maximum speed (about 3 mph), but reduced the acceleration somewhat.

In the words of *Road & Track* magazine, it was "the fastest, best sedan in the world."

Specifications

	450SEL 6.9
Engine type	V-8 cyl overhead camshafts (M 100)
Bore and stroke	107 x 95mm (4.21 x 3.74 in)
Displacement	6834 cc (417 cu in)
Power output	286 hp (DIN) @ 4250 rpm
Compression ratio	8.8:1
Torque	56 mkg @ 3000 rpm (405 ft/lb)
Fuel injection	Bosch electronic (K-Jetronic)
Engine speed at 100 km/hr	2595 rpm
Gear ratios	automatic I. 2.31:1 II. 1.46:1 III. 1.00:1
Rear axle ratio	2.65
Chassis	unit frame and body
Suspension	independent front and rear, double wishbones, diagonal-pivot swing axle, hydropneumatic, self-leveling, torsion bar stabilizers
Brakes and area	disc, vented front, solid rear, 278/279mm (10.9/11.0 in)
Wheelbase	2960mm (116.5 in)
Track, front/rear	1525/1505mm (60.0/59.3 in)
Length	5060mm (199.2 in)
Width	1870mm (73.6 in)
Height	1410mm (40mm with level adjustment) (57.1 in)
Ground clearance	150mm (5.9 in)
Tires	215/70 VR 14
Turning circle	11.8 meters (38.7 ft)
Steering type and ratio	recirculating ball (2.7 turns); servo assisted 15.6:1
Weight	1935 kg (4257 lbs)
Maximum speed	225 km/hr (140 mph)
Acceleration	7.4 sec 0-100 km/hr
Fuel consumption	16 liters, super/100 km (14.75 mpg)
Fuel tank capacity	96 liters (25.4 gallons)

Model 280SL (1974-   )

The 280SL was introduced in late 1974 as a less powerful (and consequently more economical) version of the larger engined sports cars. It shared the body and all appointments with the 350SL and 450SL fast touring models.

The engine specifications were exactly those of the other 280 cars, using the identical twin overhead camshaft six-cylinder powerplant of 185 horsepower. The 280SL weighed 45 kilograms (99 pounds) less than the 350SL and 85 kilograms (187 pounds) less than the 450SL. This still gave the smallest of the three sports cars a respectable acceleration of 9.5 seconds for the 0-100 km/hr. against the 8.8 for the 350SL and 8.5 for the 450SL. Maximum speed of the 280SL was 205 kilometers per hour (127 miles). Fuel consumption was 12.5 liters per 100 kilometers.

The 280SL model was available with the regular four-speed or five-speed transmission and the fully automatic transmission, while the other two larger-engined models had the automatic transmission and only the three-speed automatic transmission. (The 350SL had a four-speed transmission until July 1972.)

Prices and Production

The 280SL model sold in 1974 for . . . . .DM 32,445
    in 1975 for. . . . . .DM 34,335

Production of the 280SL model [107 E28] (from May/August 1974)

was in 1974	297 units
1975	1,020 units
total	1,317 units

Specifications

	280SL
Engine type	6 cyl double overhead camshafts (M 110)
Bore and stroke	86 x 78.8mm (3.41 x 3.10 in)
Displacement	2746 cc (168 cu in)
Power output	185 hp (DIN) @ 6000 rpm
Compression ratio	9:1
Torque	24.3 mkg @ 4500 rpm (175.8 ft/lb)
Fuel injection	Bosch electronic
Engine speed at 100 km/hr	3140 rpm
Gear ratios	I. 3.98:1 (14.69) or I. 3.96:1 II. 2.39:1 (8.82) II. 2.34:1 III. 1.46:1 (5.39) III. 1.43:1 IV. 1.00:1 (3.69) IV. 1.00:1 V. 0.88:1
Rear axle ratio	3.69 (for 5-speed 3.92)
Chassis	unit frame and body
Suspension	independent front and rear, double wishbones, diagonal-pivot swing axle
Brakes and area	disc, front vented, rear solid, 278/279mm (10.9/11.0 in)
Wheelbase	2460mm (96.9 in)
Track, front/rear	1452/1440mm (57.2/56.7 in)
Length	4390mm (172.8 in)
Width	1790mm (70.5 in)
Height	1300mm (51.2 in)
Ground clearance	140mm (5.5 in)
Tires	185 HR 14
Turning circle	10.34 meters (33.9 ft)
Steering type and ratio	recirculating ball (3.0 turns); servo assisted 15.6:1
Weight	1500 kg (3300 lbs)
Maximum speed	205 km/hr (127 mph); automatic: 200 km/hr (124 mph)
Acceleration	9.5 sec 0-100 km/hr
Fuel consumption	12.5 liters, super/100 km (18.75 mpg)
Fuel tank capacity	90 liters (23.8 gallons)

Model 280SLC (1974-   )

The 280SLC was brought out at the same time as the 280SL, in late 1974. As in the sports car line, this smaller engined version of the SLC model was the most economical of the three sizes available. In all appointments as well as body style and specifications, it was identical to the 350SLC and the 450SLC models.

Performance was, of course, not as brisk as that of the other two larger engined versions of the luxury coupe line, but to customers concerned with the fuel shortage and ever-increasing prices, it seemed the right answer. Weight differentials and performance figures were the same as those cited on the SL models. (The 280SLC weighed 1,550 kilograms (3,410 pound), and still attained the same maximum speed as the SL model.)

As the 280SL, this coupe also came equipped with the four- or five-speed transmission or the fully automatic transmission, while the other larger engined SLCs had only the three-speed manual and the automatic three-speed transmission.

Prices and Production

The 280SLC model sold in 1974 for . . . . .DM 37,220
    in 1975 for. . . . . .DM 39,385

Production of the 280SLC coupe [107 E28] (from May/August 1974)

was in	1974	300 units
	1975	1,312 units
	total	1,612 units

Specifications

280SLC	
Engine type	6 cyl double overhead camshafts (M 110)
Bore and stroke	86 x 78.8mm (3.41 x 3.10 in)
Displacement	2746 cc (168 cu in)
Power output	185 hp (DIN) @ 6000 rpm
Compression ratio	9:1
Torque	24.3 mkg @ 4500 rpm (175.8 ft/lb)
Fuel injection	Bosch electronic
Engine speed at 100 km/hr	3140 rpm
Gear ratios	I. 3.98:1 (14.69) or I. 3.96:1
	II. 2.39:1 (8.82) II. 2.34:1
	III. 1.46:1 (5.39) III. 1.43:1
	IV. 1.00:1 (3.69) IV. 1.00:1
	V. 0.88:1
Rear axle ratio	3.69 (for 5-speed 3.92)
Chassis	unit frame and body
Suspension	independent front and rear, double wishbones, diagonal-pivot swing axle
Brakes and area	disc, front vented, rear solid, 278/279mm (10.9/11.0 in)
Wheelbase	2820mm (111.0 in)
Track, front/rear	1452/1440mm (57.2/56.7 in)
Length	4750mm (187 in)
Width	1790mm (70.5 in)
Height	1330mm (52.4 in)
Ground clearance	140mm (5.5 in)
Tires	185 HR 14
Turning circle	11.55 meters (36.9 ft)
Steering type and ratio	recirculating ball (3.0 turns); servo assisted 15.6:1
Weight	1550 kg (3410 lbs)
Maximum speed	205 km/hr (127 mph); automatic: 200 km/hr (124 mph)
Acceleration	10.1 sec 0-100 km/hr
Fuel consumption	12.5 liters, super/100 km (18.75 mpg)
Fuel tank capacity	90 liters (23.8 gallons)

Note on Production Data

The several models with the new 123 body styles are not included in the production figures for 1975. These were:

200D	(123D)	5 units
220D	(123D)	4 units
240D	(123D)	7 units
300D	(123D)	9 units
200	(123V)	5 units
230	(123V)	9 units
250	(123V)	5 units
280	(123V)	957 units
280E	(123E)	607 units

Pre-production of all models began in July 1975 and regular production for all diesel models and the 200 and 230 models began in February 1976; of the 250 in April 1976. Regular production of the 280 and 280E models, however, began in December 1975.

The 1976 Models

At the Geneva Auto Show in March 1976 the entire line of smaller sized sedans, from the 200 to the 280E model, was introduced with new bodies, similar to the existing models. They were fitted with round headlights for the 200 through 250, and with halogen headlights for the 280E model, and bumpers had rubber guards and side strips inlets for extra protection to the body. These stronger bodies had reinforced center posts and came equipped with more padding for safety, had quieter blowers for heating and cooling systems, and an improved no-glare instrument cluster arrangement. The fuel tank was placed over the rear axle and the spare tire was resituated for greater safety and increased trunk capacity.

The completely new front suspension system gave even better directional stability to the car. Coil spring and tubular shock absorbers were utilized. The construction of the collapsible steering column was changed for greater safety. The brakes were improved and a warning light on the dashboard was provided to indicate worn brake pads on the front wheels. The altered exhaust system promised longer life.

The 230.6 model was replaced by the new 250 model. That newly designed 2,525-cubic centimeter engine had a four-bearing crankshaft with nine counterweights for greater smoothness of operation. A double Solex (4A1) downdraft carburetor was fitted. The compression ratio was 8.7 to 1, and the engine developed 129 DIN horsepower at 5,500 revolutions per minute.

The new models were the 200 with the 1,987 cc four-cylinder engine of 94 horsepower; the 230 model with the 2,307 cc four-cylinder of 109 horsepower; the 250 sedan with the 5,525 cc six-cylinder engine of 129 horsepower; the 280 model with the 2,746 cc double overhead camshaft six-cylinder engine of 156 horsepower; and the 280E with the K-jectronic fuel injection engine of 177 horsepower. The diesel-engined models were the 200D with the

1,988 cc four of 55 hp; the 220D with the 2,197 four of 60 hp; the 240D with the 2,404 cc four of 65 hp; and the 300D with the 3,005 cc five-cylinder engine developing 80 horsepower.

The 280S, 280SE and SEL, and 350SE and SEL replaced the upper range of passenger cars, orginally produced as the 250S and SE, then the 280S and SE, and 300SEL, optional with a 3.5-liter engine. More than 383,000 of these cars had been built in the seven years.

The 280 line had the 2.8-liter (2,746 cc) double overhead camshaft six-cylinder engine of 160 horsepower for the carburetor version and 185 horsepower for the fuel-injection type. The 350SE and SEL had the V-8 overhead valve engine of 3.5 liter displacement (3,499 cc) developing 200 horsepower at 5,800 rpm with a 9.5 to 1 compression ratio. These engines were practically the same as previously, but the oil could now be changed by sucking it out through the dipstick pipe. A diagnostic socket was provided to quickly check the essentials of the engine operation, and the hood could be opened wider for easier accessibility when servicing.

A synchronized four-speed transmission with floor shift was standard equipment, but a five-speed manual and an automatic four-speed transmission with torque converter were available as optional extras on these models. The cars had a slightly longer wheelbase than previously, for improved comfort and road-holding. The front axle required no maintenance. All engines had a good torque, the 350 line 29.2 mkg at 4,000 rpm; 280S 23 mkg and 280SE/SEL 24.3 mkg at 4,500; and acceleration figures were 11.5 seconds for the 280S; 10.5 seconds for the 280SE and SEL; and 9.5 seconds for the 350SE and SEL for 0-100 kilometers (62 miles) per hour.

The 280SL, 350SL, and 450SL models, two-seaters with sporty elegance and comfort, and their complimenttary coupe styles SLC, suitable for four to five persons,

were virtually unchanged from previous years. Stability of the windshield pillars had been improved and their shape kept the side windows almost completely free of road dirt in bad weather. Rear lights had also been restyled for that purpose. Wipers were rearranged to clean 70 percent of the area, and seat belts were anchored directly to the seat frame for improved safety. These models had power steering, like all S-class cars. The 280SL and SLC had the six-cylinder engine developing 185 horsepower, the 350SL and SLC the eight-cylinder 200-horsepower engine, and the 450SL and SLC the eight-cylinder engine of 225 horsepower.

The larger sedan, 450SE and 450SEL, remained unchanged from those introduced a few years before. Fitted with an improved three-speed automatic transmission, the SE accelerated from 0 to 100 kilometers (62 miles) per hour in 8.8 seconds, and the SEL in 9.3 seconds. Their maximum speeds were 210 kilometers (131 miles) per hour.

The 450SEL 6.9 sedan also remained unchanged. With the 6,834 cubic centimeter engine of 286 DIN horsepower at 4,250 rpm and torque of 56 mkg at 3,000 rpm and with a rear axle ratio of 2.65:1, the 6.9 sedan reached a maximum speed of 225 kilometers (140 miles) per hour and had an acceleration of 7.4 seconds for the 0 to 100 km (62 miles) per hour when shafting through the gears. The power-to-weight ratio of the 1,935 kilogram (4,257 lbs.) sedan was 6.8 kilogram per horsepower.

The two 600 limousine models were still available. The 6.3-liter V-8 engine developed 250 DIN horsepower (300 SAE) and gave these luxurious sedans adequate power to cruise at fantastically high speeds in greatest comfort and safety. In fact, acceleration figures of 9.7 seconds for the 0 to 100 kilometer per hour and maximum speed of 205 km (127 miles) for these 5,456-pound and 5,864-pound limousines was quite outstanding.

For 1976 the diesel engined models were designated as W 123 types. Specifications were the same as previously listed, except that the automatic transmission, optional on all models, had gear ratios of 3.98, 2.39, 1.46, and 1.00 to 1. The following specifications applied to all models:

Wheelbase — 2750mm (108.3 in)
Track, front/rear — 1488/1446mm (58.6/56.9 in)
Length — 4725mm (186.0 in)   Width — 1786mm (70.3 in)
Height — 1438mm (56.6 in)   Turning circle — 11.25 meters (36 ft)

The weights were as follows: 200D, 1375 kg (3025 lbs); 220D, 1380 kg (3036 lbs); 240D, 1385 kg (3047 lbs); 300D, 1445 kg (3179 lbs).

Specifications (for the U.S. diesel models)

	240D (OM 123)	300D (OM 123)
Engine type	4 cyl diesel, overhead camshaft	5 cyl diesel, overhead camshaft
Bore and stroke	3.58 x 3.64 in (91 x 92.4mm)	3.58 x 3.64 in (91 x 92.4mm)
Displacement	146.7 cu in (2376 cc)	183.4 cu in (2971 cc)
Power output	62 SAE hp @ 4000 rpm (65 DIN)	77 SAE hp @ 4000 rpm (80 DIN)
Compression ratio	21:1	21:1
Torque	97 ft/lb @ 2400 rpm (13.4 mkg)	115 ft/lb @ 2400 rpm (16 mkg)
Fuel injection	Bosch 4 plunger pump	Bosch 5 plunger pump
Maximum engine speed	4350 rpm	4350 rpm
Transmission	4 speed manual	4 speed automatic
Rear axle ratio	3.69:1	3.46:1
Suspension	front and rear, independent, double wishbone, diagonal swing axle	
Brakes	2 circuit hydraulic, 4 wheel power disc	
Tires	175 x 14 steel, radial	185 x 14 steel, radial
Wheelbase	108.3 in (2750mm)	108.3 in (2750mm)
Track front/rear	57.0/56.7 in (1448/1440mm)	57.0/56.7 in (1448/1440mm)
Overall length	195.5 in	195.5 in
Weight	3210 pounds	3515 pounds
Steering ratio	3.0 turns	3.0 turns
Turning circle	36.9 ft	36.9 ft
Fuel tank capacity	20.6 gallons (80 liters)	20.6 gallons (80 liters)

In the 280S, SE and SEL models the gear ratios were changed to

I. 3.90:1	automatic:	I. 3.98:1
II. 2.30:1		II. 2.39:1
III. 1.41:1		III. 1.46:1
IV. 1.00:1		IV. 1.00:1

and for the automatic transmission models the engine speed at 100 km/hr was 3,355 rpm. The maximum speed for the automatic transmission S was 185 km/hr (115 mph) and for the SE and the SEL models 195 km/hr (121 mph).

In the 350SE and SEL models the gear ratios were changed to

I. 3.96:1	automatic:	I. 2.31:1
II. 2.34:1		II. 1.46:1
III. 1.43:1		III. 1.00:1
IV. 1.00:1		

and for the automatic transmission models the engine speed at 100 km/hr was 3,295 rpm. The maximum speed for the automatic transmission car was 200 km/hr (124 mph) and the acceleration figures were 9.5 seconds 0-100 km/hr through the gears.

The 280SL and SLC models also had different gear ratios installed:

I. 3.90:1	automatic:	I. 3.98:1
II. 2.30:1		II. 2.39:1
III. 1.41:1		III. 1.46:1
IV. 1.00:1		IV. 1.00:1

and the engine speeds at 100 km/hr were 3,140 rpm and 3,380 rpm, respectively.

The 350SL and SLC models had the same specifications as before.

The 450SL and SLC models had the same automatic transmission gear ratios as those provided for the U.S. models earlier, namely 2.31, 1.46, and 1.0 to 1. The wheelbase figures were now 2,455mm (96.7 in) and acceleration was given as 8.8 seconds 0-100 km/hr, through the gears.

The 450SE and 450SEL models had the same gear ratios for the automatic transmission as the cars for the U.S. had earlier, namely 2.31, 1.46, and 1.0 to 1.

The 450SEL 6.9 model was unchanged from the previously announced sedan.

And the 600 models remained unchanged from their earlier versions as well.

Specifications

	200	230
Engine type	4 cyl overhead camshaft	4 cyl overhead camshaft
Bore and stroke	87 x 83.6mm (3.43 x 3.29 in)	93.75 x 83.6mm (3.69 x 3.29 in)
Displacement	1987 cc (121.27 cu in)	2307 cc (140.8 cu in)
Power output	94 hp (DIN) @ 4800 rpm (105 hp SAE)	109 hp (DIN) @ 4800 rpm
Compression ratio	9.0:1	9.0:1
Torque	16.1 mkg @ 3000 rpm	18.9 mkg @ 3000 rpm
Carburetion	Stromberg crossdraft, type 175 CD	
Engine speed at 100 km/hr	3395 rpm	3195 rpm
Gear ratios	I. 3.90:1 automatic II. 2.30:1 III. 1.41:1 IV. 1.00:1	I. 3.98:1 II. 2.39:1 III. 1.46:1 IV. 1.00:1
Rear axle ratio	3.46	3.69
Chassis	unit frame and body	unit frame and body
Suspension	independent front and rear, with coil springs, diagonal-pivot swing axle, anti-sway bars	
Brakes and area	dual circuit disc, power assisted, front wheel pad wear indicator	
Wheelbase	2795mm (110.0 in)	2795mm (110.0 in)
Track, front/rear	1488/1446mm (58.6/56.9 in)	1488/1446mm (58.6/56.9 in)
Length	4725mm (186.0 in)	4725mm (186.0 in)
Width	1786mm (70.3 in)	1786mm (70.3 in)
Height	1438mm (56.6 in)	1438mm (56.6 in)
Ground clearance	175mm (6.9 in)	175mm (6.9 in)
Tires	175 SR 14	175 SR 14
Turning circle	11.25 meters (36 ft)	11.25 meters (36 ft)
Steering type and ratio	recirculating ball (4.0 turns); servo assisted	
Weight	1445 kg (3179 lbs)	1350 kg (2970 lbs)
Maximum speed	148 km/hr automatic: 143 km/hr	170 km/hr automatic: 165 km/hr
Acceleration	19.9 sec 0-100 km/hr automatic: 16 sec	13.7 sec 0-100 km/hr automatic: 13.9 sec
Fuel consumption	10.8 liters/100 km	11.7 liters/100 km
Fuel tank capacity	65 liters (17.2 gallons)	65 liters (17.2 gallons)

250	280	280E
6 cyl overhead camshaft	6 cyl double overhead camshaft	6 cyl double overhead camshaft
86 x 72.45mm	86 x 78.8mm (3.39 x 3.10 in)	86 x 78.8mm
2525 cc	2746 cc (167.6 cu in)	2746 cc
129 hp (DIN) @ 5500 rpm	156 hp (DIN) @ 5500 rpm	177 hp (DIN) @ 6000 rpm
8.7:1	8.7:1	8.7:1
20.0 mkg @ 3500 rpm	22.7 mkg @ 4000 rpm	23.8 mkg @ 45000 rpm
Solex dual compound downdraft, type 4A1		mechanical fuel injection
3195 rpm; automatic: 3275 rpm	3065 rpm; automatic: 3155 rpm	3065 rpm

250		280	280E
I. 3.90:1	automatic	I. 3.98:1	
II. 2.30:1		II. 2.39:1	
III. 1.41:1		III. 1.46:1	
IV. 1.00:1		IV. 1.00:1	

250	280	280E
3.69	3.54	3.55
unit frame and body	unit frame and body	unit frame and body
independent front and rear, with coil springs, diagonal-pivot swing axle, anti-sway bars		
dual circuit disc, power assisted, front wheel pad wear indicator		
2795mm (110.0 in)	2795mm (110.0 in)	2795mm (110.0 in)
1488/1446mm (58.6/56.9 in)	1488/1446mm (58.6/56.9 in)	1488/1446mm (58.6/56.9 in)
4725mm (186.0 in)	4725mm (186.0 in)	4725mm (186.0 in)
1786mm (70.3 in)	1786mm (70.3 in)	1786mm (70.3 in)
1438mm (56.6 in)	1438mm (56.6 in)	1438mm (56.6 in)
175mm (6.9 in)	175mm (6.9 in)	175mm (6.9 in)
175 SR 14	195/70 HR 14	195/70 HR 14
11.25 meters (36 ft)	11.25 meters (36 ft)	11.25 meters (36 ft)
recirculating ball (4.0 turns); servo assisted		
1360 kg (2992 lbs)	1455 kg (3201 lbs)	1460 kg (3212 lbs)
180 km/hr automatic: 175 km/hr	190 km/hr automatic: 185 km/hr	200 km/hr automatic: 195 km/hr
11.5 sec 0-100 km/hr automatic: 12.4 sec	10.6 sec 0-100 km/hr automatic: 11.3 sec	9.9 sec 0-100 km/hr automatic: 10.8 sec
11.8 liters/100 km	12.5 liters/100 km	12.5 liters/100 km
65 liters (17.2 gallons)	80 liters (20.6 gallons)	80 liters (20.6 gallons)

1976 Models in the U.S.

Ten models were available in the United States in 1976. The gasoline-engined four-cylinder 230 sedan, the six-cylinder 280 sedan and 280C coupe, and the larger bodied 280S sedan; in the V-8 engined models, the 450SE and the 450SEL sedans, the two-seater 450SL with both soft and hard top, and the four-seater 450SLC coupe. In the diesel-engined line, the 240D with the four-cylinder engine and the 300D with the five-cylinder, were sold in this country.

Sales of these two diesel-engined automobiles were only limited by their short supply, yet still about 40 percent of all passenger car sales in 1975 by Mercedes-Benz in this country were of these models. One of the improvements in the 240D and 300D was a larger fuel tank to hold 80 liters (20.6 gallons) to give the 240D a driving range of 638 miles and the 300D 576 miles, using the U.S. Government Enviromental Protection Agency figures for fuel consumption.

Engineering changes for the year included an improved, yet simpler fuel injection system for all cars with the V-8 engines, and a more sophisticated cruise control system as well as a newly developed automatic climate control system. The cruise control device was standard on all models except the 230 and 240D. The climate control was standard equipment on the 280S, 450SE, and 450SEL cars. Bosch K-jetronic fuel injection was used on the 4.5-liter engines. A hydraulic valve adjustment system was also used on all V-8 engines, reducing service requirements, as well as a new electronic ignition system with breakerless distrubutor.

Specifications

	230	280
Engine type	4 cyl overhead camshaft 5 main bearings	6 cyl double overhead camshaft 7 main bearings
Horsepower @ rpm	93 @ 4800 (84 @ 4500 Cal)	120 @ 4800
Torque ft/lb @ rpm	125 @ 2500 (122 Cal)	143 @ 2800
Bore x stroke in	3.69 x 3.29	3.39 x 3.10
Displacement cu in	140.8	167.6
Maximum engine speed	6000 rpm	6500 rpm
Compression ratio	8.0:1	8.0:1
Transmission	4 speed automatic with torque converter (all models)	
Rear axle ratio	3.92:1	3.69:1
Suspension, front	Independent, double wishbones, anti-dive control. Wheels	
Suspension, rear	Independent, diagonal swing axle, anti-lift control. Wheels	
Tires and rims	185 x 14 steel belted radial tires, (standard all models)	
	5.5J x 14	6J x 14
Braking system	2 circuit hydraulic; 4 wheel power disc brakes (all models)	
Wheelbase in	108.3	108.3
Track, front/rear	57.0/56.7	57.0/56.7
Overall length in	195.5	195.5
Curb weight lbs	3185	3520
Fuel tank capacity	20.6 gal with 2.4 gallons reserve tank (all models)	
Steering turns	3.0	3.0
Turning circle ft	36.9	36.9
Trunk capacity cu ft	17.5	17.5
Battery capacity	12/66 amp/hrs	12/55

280C	280S	450SE / 450SEL / 450SL / 450SLC			
6 cyl double overhead camshaft	6 cyl double overhead camshaft	V-8 cyl overhead camshafts, fuel injection			
7 main bearings	7 main bearings	5 main bearings			
120 @ 4800	120 @ 4800	180 @ 4750			
143 @ 2800	143 @ 2800	220 @ 3000			
3.39 x 3.10	3.39 x 3.10	3.62 x 3.35			
167.6	167.6	275.8			
6500 rpm	6500 rpm	5800 rpm			
8.0:1	8.0:1	8.0:1			
4 speed automatic with torque converter		3 speed automatic with torque converter			
3.69:1	3.69:1	3.07:1			
il springs, stabilizer bar, single tube shock absorbers, gas pressurized					
il springs, stabilizer bar, single tube shock absorbers					
		205 x 14 steel belted radial			
6J x 14	6J x 14	6.5J x 14			
		2 circuit hydraulic; 4 wheel power disc brakes; front discs are ventilated (all models)			
		450SE	450SEL	450SL	450SLC
108.3	112.8	112.8	116.7	96.9	111.0
57.0/56.7	59.9/59.3	59.9/59.3	59.9/59.3	57.2/56.7	57.2/56.7
195.5	205.5	205.5	209.4	182.3	196.4
3550	3905	4105	4135	3795	3905
		25.4 gal with 3.4 gallons reserve tank (also sedan models)		23.8 gal	23.8 gal
3.0	2.7	2.7	2.7	3.0	3.0
36.9	38.0	38.0	38.0	34.4	38.3
19.3	18.2	18.2	18.2	8.6	10.3
12/55	12/55	12/66	12/66	12/88	12/88

The 1977 Models

For the model year 1977, eight different sedans were offered in the United States. The 230, the four-cylinder gasoline engined car, was sold only in the eastern half of the country, and the 280E had the six-cylinder double overhead camshaft fuel injection engine. The 240D and 300D shared the bodies with these models. Unchanged from the previous year were the larger four-door sedans, the 280SE with the fuel-injected double overhead camshaft engine, the longer wheelbase sedan 450SEL with the V-8 engine, as well as the 450SL coupe-roadster, and the 450SLC coupe.

The specifications for the 1977 cars were identical with those listed for the 1976 models except for the following: the 230 model had an engine of 86 hp at 4,800 rpm and a torque of 116 ft/lb. (16.8 mkg) at 3,000 rpm. Rear axle ratio was 3.69:1 and 175 SR x 14 tires were fitted. The 280E model had the 142 hp at 5,750 rpm (California 137 hp) engine with a torque of 149 ft/lb. (Cal 142) at 4,600 rpm, a rear axle ratio of 3.54:1 and had 195/70

HR x 14 tires mounted. The 300D had also 195/70 HR x 14 tires. The body specifications for 230, 280E, 240D, and 300D models were alike.

Wheelbase — 110.0 in. (2,795mm)
Track, front/rear — 58.6/56.9 in. (1488/1446mm)
Length — 190.9 in. (4,848mm)
Fuel tank capacity 21.1 gal. (80 liter)
Steering ratio 2.7 turns
Turning circle 37 ft. (11.29 meters)

The weight of the 230 sedan was 3,195 lbs (1,450 kg) and that of the 280E 3,530 lbs. (1,600 kg).

The 280SE had an engine of 142 hp at 5,750 rpm (California 137 hp) and torque of 149 ft/lb. at 4,600 rpm (21.4 mkg) (California 142 and 20.5). The weight of the 280SE was 3,905 lbs. (1,770 kg), the 450SEL 4,080 lbs. (1,850 kg), the 450SL 3,815 lbs. (1,730 kg), and the 450SLC 3,860 lbs. (1,750 kg).

Model Offerings

These random offerings are given merely to emphasize the fact that only carefully selected models of the large variety available from the factory were sold in the United States. For example, in 1976 only 10 models were marketed here while the factory offered a total of 27 models (actually 41 were listed, counting the 2 styles 115/114 and 123 of the smaller cars, the longer wheelbase versions, and three versions of the 600 limousine).

For 1966 Daimler-Benz offered for sale:

200	2.0 liter gasoline	4 cyl	95 hp DIN
200D	2.0 liter diesel	4 cyl	55 hp DIN
230	2.3 liter gasoline	6 cyl	105 hp DIN
230S	2.3 liter gasoline	6 cyl	120 hp DIN
250S	2.5 liter gasoline	6 cyl	130 hp DIN
250SE	2.5 liter gasoline	6 cyl	150 hp DIN
220SE coupe and convertible	2.2 liter gasoline	6 cyl	120 hp DIN
250SE coupe and convertible	2.5 liter gasoline	6 cyl	150 hp DIN
300SEb	3.0 liter gasoline	6 cyl	170 hp DIN
300SEL	3.0 liter gasoline	6 cyl	170 hp DIN
300SE coupe and convertible	3.0 liter gasoline	6 cyl	170 hp DIN
230SL	2.3 liter gasoline	6 cyl	150 hp DIN
600	6.3 liter gasoline	8 cyl	250 hp DIN
600 pullman	6.3 liter gasoline	8 cyl	250 hp DIN

For 1970 the following models were sold in the U.S.

220	2.2 liter gasoline	4 cyl	116 hp SAE
220D	2.2 liter diesel	4 cyl	65 hp SAE
250	2.5 liter gasoline	6 cyl	146 hp SAE
250C	2.8 liter gasoline	6 cyl	157 hp SAE
280S	2.8 liter gasoline	6 cyl	157 hp SAE
280SE	2.8 liter gasoline	6 cyl	180 hp SAE
280SEL	2.8 liter gasoline	6 cyl	180 hp SAE
280SE coupe and convertible	2.8 liter gasoline	6 cyl	180 hp SAE
280SL	2.8 liter gasoline	6 cyl	180 hp SAE
300SEL	2.8 liter gasoline	6 cyl	180 hp SAE
300SEL 6.3	6.3 liter gasoline	8 cyl	300 hp SAE
600 5 passenger	6.3 liter gasoline	8 cyl	300 hp SAE
600 7 passenger	6.3 liter gasoline	8 cyl	300 hp SAE

For 1976 Daimler-Benz offered for sale:

200D	2.0 liter diesel	4 cyl	55 hp DIN
220D	2.2 liter diesel	4 cyl	60 hp DIN
240D	2.4 liter diesel	4 cyl	65 hp DIN
240D 3.0	3.0 liter diesel	5 cyl	80 hp DIN
200	2.0 liter gasoline	4 cyl	95 hp DIN
230.4	2.3 liter gasoline	4 cyl	110 hp DIN
230.6	2.3 liter gasoline	6 cyl	120 hp DIN
250	2.8 liter gasoline	6 cyl	130 hp DIN
280	2.8 liter gasoline	6 cyl	160 hp DIN
280E	2.8 liter gasoline	6 cyl	185 hp DIN
250C	2.8 liter gasoline	6 cyl	130 hp DIN
280C	2.8 liter gasoline	6 cyl	160 hp DIN
280CE	2.8 liter gasoline	6 cyl	185 hp DIN
280S	2.8 liter gasoline	6 cyl	160 hp DIN
280SE	2.8 liter gasoline	6 cyl	185 hp DIN
280SEL	2.8 liter gasoline	6 cyl	185 hp DIN
350SE	3.5 liter gasoline	8 cyl	200 hp DIN
350SEL	3.5 liter gasoline	8 cyl	200 hp DIN
450SE	4.5 liter gasoline	8 cyl	225 hp DIN
450SEL	4.5 liter gasoline	8 cyl	225 hp DIN
450SEL 6.9	6.9 liter gasoline	8 cyl	286 hp DIN
280SL	2.8 liter gasoline	6 cyl	185 hp DIN
350SL	3.5 liter gasoline	8 cyl	200 hp DIN
450SL	4.5 liter gasoline	8 cyl	225 hp DIN
280SLC	2.8 liter gasoline	6 cyl	185 hp DIN
350SLC	3.5 liter gasoline	8 cyl	200 hp DIN
450SLC	4.5 liter gasoline	8 cyl	225 hp DIN

For 1976 the following models were sold in the U.S.

240D	2.4 liter diesel	4 cyl	62 hp SAE
300D	3.0 liter diesel	5 cyl	77 hp SAE
230	2.3 liter gasoline	4 cyl	93 hp SAE (Cal. 85)
280	2.8 liter gasoline	6 cyl	120 hp SAE
280C	2.8 liter gasoline	6 cyl	120 hp SAE
280S	2.8 liter gasoline	6 cyl	120 hp SAE
450SE	4.5 liter gasoline	8 cyl	180 hp SAE
450SEL	4.5 liter gasoline	8 cyl	180 hp SAE
450SL	4.5 liter gasoline	8 cyl	180 hp SAE
450SLC	4.5 liter gasoline	8 cyl	180 hp SAE

1946-1975 Models Index

For clarity, only the basic types are listed here. Model number in **bold face**, page number in light face.

170Vb

450SEL 6.9

1946-75 Production Totals

Year	MB Pass. Car Production	MB Pass. Car Sales in US	% of MB Sales to Total Imp. Car Sales	Total Imp. Car Sales in US
1946	214			
1947	1,045			
1948	5,116			
1949	17,417			
1950	33,906	13 ⎫ import figures		⎫ Start up
1951	42,222	18 ⎪ for calendar years		⎪ through
1952	36,824	253 ⎬ no sales figure		⎬ 12/10/57
1953	34,975	421 ⎭ available		1,348 MB-
1954	48,816			Car Sales
1955	63,683			Retail &
1956	69,601			Tourist
1957	80,899			
1958	99,209	7,404		
1959	108,440	12,071		
1960	122,684	12,254		
1961	137,431	12,625		
1962	146,393	12,947		339,160
1963	153,182	11,688	3.03	385,624
1964	165,532	11,867	2.45	484,131
1965	174,007	12,117	2.13	569,415
1966	191,625	16,162	2.46	658,123
1967	200,470	20,691	2.66	779,220
1968	216,284	24,553	2.49	985,767
1969	256,713	26,193	2.47	1,061,617
1970	280,419	29,108	2.36	1,230,961
1971	284,230	35,156	2.36	1,487,613
1972	323,878	41,556	2.72	1,529,402
1973	331,682	41,865	2.43	1,719,913
1974	340,006	38,170	2.79	1,369,148
1975	350,098	45,159		

Engine Designations

Gasoline Engines (designated M=Motor)

M 136	4 cyl	1.7 and 1.8 liter	carburetor	1946-57
M 121	4 cyl	1.9 and 2.0 liter	carburetor	1953-68
M 115	4 cyl	2.0 and 2.2 and 2.3 liter	carburetor	1967-
M 180	6 cyl	2.2 and 2.3 liter	carburetor	1951-76
M 127	6 cyl	2.2 and 2.3 liter	fuel injection	1958-67
M 108	6 cyl	2.5 liter	carburetor	1965-69
M 129	6 cyl	2.5 liter	fuel injection	1965-68
M 114	6 cyl	2.5 liter	carburetor and fuel injection	1967-72
M 123	6 cyl	2.5 liter	carburetor	1976-
M 130	6 cyl	2.8 liter	carburetor and fuel injection	1967-76
M 110	6 cyl	2.8 liter	carburetor and fuel injection	1972-
M 186	6 cyl	3.0 liter	carburetor	1951-67
M 188	6 cyl	3.0 liter	carburetor	1952-55
M 198	6 cyl	3.0 liter	fuel injection	1954-63
M 199	6 cyl	3.0 liter	fuel injection	1955-58
M 189	6 cyl	3.0 liter	fuel injection	1957-67
M 116	8 cyl	3.5 liter	fuel injection	1969-
M 117	8 cyl	4.5 liter	fuel injection	1971-
M 100	8 cyl	6.3 and 6.9 liter	fuel injection	1964-

Diesel Engines (designated OM=Oel Motor)

OM 636	4 cyl	1.7 and 1.8 liter	injection	1949-61
OM 621	4 cyl	1.9 and 2.0 liter	injection	1958-68
OM 615	4 cyl	2.0 and 2.2 liter	injection	1967-
OM 616	4 cyl	2.4 liter	injection	1973-
OM 617	5 cyl	3.0 liter	injection	1974-

Engine Production Details

Comments:

lo comp: *lower compression engine*
sedan: *four-door sedan*
cp/con: *coupe and convertible*
roadster: *roadster model*

autom: *for automatic transmission model*
cp/lt met: *light metal coupe*
lt met dif: *light metal differential*
K-Jet: *K-Jetronic fuel injection*

Diesel Engines

Construction Design Number	Cylinders	Bore cc	Stroke cc	Displacement cc	Compression Ratio	Horsepower DIN	Revolutions Per Minute	Model	Manufacturing Designation	Built from - to	Comments
636.915	4	73.5 x 100.0		1,697	19:1	38	3,200	170D	W136	May 1949 to May 1950	
636.916	4	75.0 x 100.0		1,767	19:1	40	3,200	170Da	W136	May 1950 to Apr 1952	
636.916	4	75.0 x 100.0		1,767	19:1	40	3,200	170Dc	W136	May 1952 to Oct 1953	
636.918	4	75.0 x 100.0		1,767	19:1	40	3,200	170D-S	W191	Jan 1952 to Aug 1953	
636.930	4	75.0 x 100.0		1,767	19:1	43	3,500	180D	W120	Oct 1953 to Jul 1959	
636.930	4	75.0 x 100.0		1,767	19:1	43	3,500	180Db	W120	Jul 1959 to Aug 1961	
636.931	4	75.0 x 100.0		1,767	19:1	40	3,200	170S-D	W136	Jul 1953 to Sep 1955	
621.910	4	85.0 x 83.6		1,897	21:1	50	4,000	190D	W121	Aug 1958 to Jul 1959	
621.910	4	85.0 x 83.6		1,897	21:1	50	4,000	190Db	W121	Jun 1959 to Sep 1961	
621.912	4	87.0 x 83.6		1,988	21:1	55	4,200	190Dc	W110	Apr 1961 to Aug 1965	
621.914	4	87.0 x 83.6		1,988	21:1	48	3,800	180Dc	W120	Jun 1961 to Oct 1962	
621.918	4	87.0 x 83.6		1,988	21:1	55	4,200	200D	W110	Jun 1965 to Feb 1968	
615.912	4	87.0 x 92.4		2,197	21:1	60	4,200	220D	W115	Jul 1967	
615.913	4	87.0 x 83.6		1,988	21:1	55	4,200	200D	W115	Oct 1967	
615.940	4	87.0 x 83.6		1,988	21:1	55	4,200	200D	W123	Jan 1976	
615.941	4	87.0 x 92.4		2,197	21:1	60	4,200	220D	W123	Jan 1976	
616.912	4	91.0 x 92.4		2,404	21:1	65	4,200	240D	W123	Jan 1976	
616.916	4	91.0 x 92.4		2,404	21:1	65	4,200	240D	W115	Aug 1973	
617.910	5	91.0 x 92.4		3,005	21:1	80	4,000	240D 3.0	W115	Sep 1974	
617.911	5	91.0 x 92.4		3,005	21:1	80	4,000	300D	W123	Jan 1976	

Gasoline Engines

Construction Design Number	Cylinders	Bore cc	Stroke cc	Displacement cc	Compression Ratio	Horsepower DIN	Revolutions Per Minute	Model	Manufacturing Designation	Built from - to	Comments
136.920	4	73.5 x 100.0	1,697	6.5:1	38	3,600	170V	W136	Jun 1946 to May 1950	
136.921	4	73.5 x 100.0	1,697	6.5:1	38	3,600	170V	W136	Jun 1946 to May 1950	
136.922	4	75.0 x 100.0	1,767	6.5:1	52	4,000	170S	W136	May 1949 to Feb 1952	
136.922	4	75.0 x 100.0	1,767	6.5:1	52	4,000	170Sb	W191	Feb 1952 to Aug 1953	
136.923	4	75.0 x 100.0	1,767	6.5:1	45	3,600	170Va	W136	May 1950 to Apr 1952	
136.923	4	75.0 x 100.0	1,767	6.5:1	45	3,600	170Vb	W136	May 1952 to Aug 1953	
136.925	4	75.0 x 100.0	1,767	6.7:1	52	4,000	180	W120	Jul 1953 to Jun 1957	
136.926	4	75.0 x 100.0	1,767	6.5:1	45	3.600	170S-V	W136	Jul 1953 to Feb 1955	
121.920	4	85.0 x 83.6	1,897	7.5:1	75	4,600	190	W121	Mar 1956 to Aug 1959	
121.920	4	85.0 x 83.6	1,897	8.5:1	80	4,800	190b	W121	Jun 1959 to Aug 1961	
121.921	4	85.0 x 83.6	1,897	8.8:1	105	5,700	190SL	W121	Jun 1953 to Jul 1961	
121.923	4	85.0 x 83.6	1,897	6.9:1	65	4,500	180a	W120	Jun 1957 to Jul 1959	
121.923	4	85.0 x 83.6	1,897	7.0:1	68	4,400	180b	W120	Jul 1959 to Aug 1961	
121.924	4	85.0 x 83.6	1,897	8.7:1	80	5,000	190c	W110	Apr 1961 to Aug 1965	
121.927	4	85.0 x 83.6	1,897	7.0:1	68	4,400	180c	W120	Jun 1961 to Oct 1962	
121.928	4	85.0 x 83.6	1,897	8.7:1	105	5,700	190SL	W121	May 1961 to Feb 1963	
121.940	4	87.0 x 83.6	1,988	9.0:1	95	5,200	200	W110	Jun 1965 to Feb 1968	
180.920	6	80.0 x 72.8	2,195	6.5:1	80	4,600	220	W187	Apr 1951 to Aug 1955	
180.921	6	80.0 x 72.8	2,195	7.6:1	85	4,800	219	W105	May 1955 to Jul 1959	
180.921	6	80.0 x 72.8	2,195	7.6:1	85	4,800	220a	W180	Jan 1954 to Apr 1956	
180.924	6	80.0 x 72.8	2,195	7.6:1	100	4,800	220S	W180	Apr 1956 to Jul 1959	
180.940	6	80.0 x 72.8	2,195	8.7:1	95	4,800	220b	W111	May 1959 to Aug 1965	
180.941	6	80.0 x 72.8	2,195	8.7:1	110	5,000	220Sb	W111	May 1959 to Jul 1965	
180.945	6	82.0 x 72.8	2,306	9.0:1	105	5,200	230	W110	Jul 1965 to Jun 1966	
180.947	6	82.0 x 72.8	2,306	9.0:1	120	5,400	230S	W111	Jul 1965 to Jan 1968	
180.949	6	82.0 x 72.8	2,306	9.0:1	120	5,200	230	W110	Jul 1966 to Dec 1967	
180.954	6	81.75 x 72.8	2,292	8.7:1	120	5,400	230.6	W114	Sep 1967	
180.955	6	81.75 x 72.8	2,292	7.2:1	106	5,300	230.6	W114	Sep 1967	lo comp
127.980	6	80.0 x 72.8	2,195	8.7:1	115	4,800	220SE	W128	Apr 1958 to Aug 1959	sedan
127.981	6	82.0 x 72.8	2,195	9.3:1	150	5,500	230SL	W113	Mar 1963 to Jan 1967	
127.982	6	80.0 x 72.8	2,195	8.7:1	120	4,800	220SEb	W111	Aug 1959 to Aug 1965	sedan
127.983	6	80.0 x 72.8	2,195	8.7:1	115	4,800	220SE	W128	Jul 1958 to Nov 1960	cp/con
127.984	6	80.0 x 72.8	2,195	8.7:1	120	4,800	220SEb	W111	Sep 1960 to Oct 1965	cp/con

Gasoline Engines

Construction Design Number	Cylinders	Bore cc x Stroke cc	Displacement	Compression Ratio	Horsepower DIN	Revolutions Per Minute	Model	Manufacturing Designation	Built from - to	Comments
115.920	4	87.0 x 92.4	2,197	9.0:1	105	5,000	220/8	W115	Oct 1967 to Jul 1973	
115.923	4	87.0 x 83.6	1,988	9.0:1	95	4,800	200	W115	Oct 1967	
115.924	4	87.0 x 92.4	2,197	7.8:1	90	5,000	220/8	W115	Oct 1967 to Jul 1973	lo comp
115.926	4	87.0 x 83.6	1,988	8.0:1	85	5,000	200	W115	Oct 1967	lo comp
115.938	4	87.0 x 83.6	1,987	9.0:1	94	4,800	200	W123	Jan 1976	
115.939	4	87.0 x 83.6	1,987	8.0:1	84	4,800	200	W123	Jan 1976	lo comp
115.951	4	93.75 x 83.6	2,307	9.0:1	110	4,800	230.4	W115	Aug 1973	
115.954	4	93.75 x 83.6	2,307	9.0:1	109	4,800	230	W123	Jan 1976	
108.920	6	82.0 x 78.8	2,496	9.0:1	130	5,400	250S	W108	Jul 1965 to Mar 1969	
108.924	6	82.0 x 78.8	2,496	7.7:1	115	5,400	250S	W108	Jul 1965 to Mar 1969	lo comp
129.980	6	82.0 x 78.8	2,496	9.3:1	150	5,500	250SE	W108	Aug 1965 to Jan 1968	
129.980	6	82.0 x 78.8	2,496	9.3:1	150	5,500	250SE	W111	Apr 1966 to Dec 1967	
129.981	6	82.0 x 78.8	2,496	9.3:1	150	5,500	250SE	W111	Aug 1965 to Apr 1966	
129.982	6	82.0 x 78.8	2,496	9.5:1	150	5,500	250SL	W113	Nov 1966 to Jan 1968	
114.920	6	82.0 x 78.8	2,496	9.0:1	130	5,400	250/8	W114	Jul 1967 to Apr 1972	
114.923	6	82.0 x 78.8	2,496	7.7:1	115	5,400	250C/8	W114	Oct 1968 to Apr 1972	lo comp
114.980	6	82.0 x 78.8	2,496	9.5:1	150	5,500	250CE/8	W114	Oct 1968 to Apr 1972	
114.981	6	82.0 x 78.8	2,496	7.1:1	130	5,500	250CE/8	W114	Oct 1968 to Apr 1972	lo comp
123.920	6	86.0 x 72.45	2,525	8.7:1	129	5,500	250	W123	Jan 1976	
130.920	6	86.5 x 78.8	2,778	9.0:1	140	5,200	280S	W108	Nov 1967 to Sep 1972	
130.921	6	86.5 x 78.8	2,778	7.8:1	125	5,200	280S	W108	Nov 1967 to Sep 1972	lo comp
130.923	6	86.5 x 78.8	2,778	9.0:1	140	5,200	250	W114	Jul 1970 to Aug 1972	
130.923	6	86.5 x 78.8	2,778	9.0:1	130	5,000	250C	W114	Jun 1972	
130.933	6	86.5 x 78.8	2,778	7.6:1	118	5,000	250C	W114	Jun 1972	lo comp
130.980	6	86.5 x 78.8	2,778	9.5:1	160	5,500	280SE	W108	Nov 1967 to Sep 1972	
130.980	6	86.5 x 78.8	2,778	9.5:1	160	5,500	280SEL	W108	Jan 1968 to Mar 1971	
130.980	6	86.5 x 78.8	2,778	9.5:1	160	5,500	280SE	W111	Nov 1967 to Feb 1971	
130.981	6	86.5 x 78.8	2,778	9.5:1	170	5,750	300SEL	W109	Dec 1967 to Jan 1970	
130.983	6	86.5 x 78.8	2,778	9.5:1	170	5,750	280SL	W113	Nov 1967 to Mar 1971	
130.984	6	86.5 x 78.8	2,778	7.8:1	140	5,250	280SE	W108	Nov 1967 to Sep 1972	lo comp
130.984	6	86.5 x 78.8	2,778	7.8:1	140	5,250	280SEL	W108	Jan 1968 to Mar 1971	lo comp
130.984	6	86.5 x 78.8	2,778	7.8:1	140	5,250	280SE	W111	Nov 1967 to Feb 1971	lo comp

Gasoline Engines

Construction Design Number	Cylinders	Bore cc	Stroke cc	Displacement cc	Compression Ratio	Horsepower DIN	Revolutions Per Minute	Model	Manufacturing Designation	Built from - to	Comments
186.920	6	85.0 x 88.0		2,996	6.4:1	115	4,600	300	W186	Nov 1951 to Mar 1954	
186.920	6	85.0 x 88.0		2,996	7.5:1	125	4,500	300b	W186	Mar 1954 to Jul 1955	
186.921	6	85.0 x 88.0		2,996	7.5:1	125	4,500	300c	W186	Jul 1955 to Aug 1967	
188.920	6	85.0 x 88.0		2,996	7.8:1	150	5,000	300S	W188	Jan 1952 to Jul 1955	
199.980	6	85.0 x 88.0		2,996	8.5:1	175	5,300	300Sc	W188	Jul 1955 to Apr 1958	
189.980	6	85.0 x 88.0		2,996	8.5:1	160	5,400	300d	W189	Aug 1957 to Mar 1962	autom
189.981	6	85.0 x 88.0		2,996	8.5:1	160	5,300	300d	W189	Aug 1957 to Mar 1962	autom
189.984	6	85.0 x 88.0		2,996	8.7:1	160	5,000	300SE	W112	Jul 1961 to Nov 1963	sedan
189.985	6	85.0 x 88.0		2,996	8.7:1	160	5,000	300SE	W112	Sep 1961 to Nov 1963	cp/con
189.986	6	85.0 x 88.0		2,996	8.8:1	170	5,400	300SE	W112	Oct 1963 to Jul 1965	sedan
189.987	6	85.0 x 88.0		2,996	8.8:1	170	5,400	300SE	W112	Oct 1963 to Dec 1967	cp/con
189.988	6	85.0 x 88.0		2,996	8.8:1	170	5,400	300SEL	W109	Aug 1965 to Dec 1967	
189.989	6	85.0 x 88.0		2,996	8.8:1	170	5,400	300SEb	W108	Aug 1965 to Dec 1967	
198.980	6	85.0 x 88.0		2.996	8.5:1	215	5,800	300SL	W198	Sep 1954 to May 1957	cp
198.980	6	85.0 x 88.0		2,996	8.5:1	215	5,800	300SL	W198	May 1957 to Mar 1962	roadster
198.981	6	85.0 x 88.0		2,996	8.5:1	215	5,800	300SL	W198	Sep 1954 to May 1957	cp/lt met
198.982	6	85.0 x 88.0		2,996	8.5:1	215	5,800	300SL	W198	Mar 1962 to Feb 1963	roadster lt met dif
116.980	8-V	92.0 x 65.8		3,499	9.5:1	200	5,800	280SE 3.5	W111	Aug 1969 to Jul 1971	
116.980	8-V	92.0 x 65.8		3,499	9.5:1	200	5,800	280SE/SEL 3.5	W108	Mar 1971 to Aug 1972	
116.981	8-V	92.0 x 65.8		3,499	9.5:1	200	5,800	300SEL 3.5	W109	Sep 1969 to Sep 1972	
116.982	8-V	92.0 x 65.8		3,499	9.5:1	200	5,800	350SLC	W107	Aug 1971 to Feb 1976	
116.982	8-V	92.0 x 65.8		3,499	9.5:1	200	5,800	350SL	W107	Feb 1971 to Feb 1976	
116.983	8-V	92.0 x 65.8		3,499	9.5:1	200	5,800	350SE	W116	Sep 1972 to Feb 1976	
116.983	8-V	92.0 x 65.8		3,499	9.5:1	200	5,800	350SEL	W116	Nov 1973 to Feb 1976	
116.984	8-V	92.0 x 65.8		3,499	9.5:1	200	5,800	350SL/SLC	W107	Feb 1976	K-Jet
116.985	8-V	92.0 x 65.8		3,499	9.5:1	200	5,800	350SE/SEL	W116	Feb 1976	K-Jet
116.990	8-V	92.0 x 65.8		3,499	8.0:1	180	5,500	280SE 3.5	W111	Aug 1969 to Jul 1971	lo comp
116.990	8-V	92.0 x 65.8		3,499	8.0:1	180	5,500	280SE/SEL 3.5	W108	Mar 1971 to Aug 1972	lo comp
116.991	8-V	92.0 x 65.8		3,499	8.0:1	180	5,500	300SEL 3.5	W109	Sep 1969 to Aug 1972	lo comp
116.992	8-V	92.0 x 65.8		3,499	8.0:1	180	5,500	350SL	W107	Feb 1971 to Feb 1976	lo comp
116.992	8-V	92.0 x 65.8		3,499	8.0:1	180	5,500	350SLC	W107	Aug 1971 to Feb 1976	lo comp
116.993	8-V	92.0 x 65.8		3,499	8.0:1	180	5,500	350SE	W116	Sep 1972 to Feb 1976	lo comp
116.993	8-V	92.0 x 65.8		3,499	8.0:1	180	5,500	350SEL	W116	Nov 1973 to Feb 1976	lo comp

Gasoline Engines

Construction Design Number	Cylinders	Bore cc	Stroke cc	Displacement cc	Compression Ratio	Horsepower DIN	Revolutions Per Minute	Model	Manufacturing Designation	Built from - to	Comments
110.921	6	86.0 x 78.8		2,746	9.0:1	160	5,500	280	W114	Apr 1972	
110.921	6	86.0 x 78.8		2,746	9.0:1	160	5,500	280C	W114	Jun 1972	
110.922	6	86.0 x 78.8		2,746	9.0:1	160	5,500	280S	W116	Aug 1972	
110.923	6	86.0 x 78.8		2,746	8.7:1	156	5,500	280	W123	Jan 1976	
110.931	6	86.0 x 78.8		2,746	8.0:1	145	5,500	280	W114	Apr 1972	
110.931	6	86.0 x 78.8		2,746	8.0:1	145	5,500	280C	W114	Jun 1972	lo comp
110.932	6	86.0 x 78.8		2,746	8.0:1	145	5,500	280S	W116	Aug 1972	lo comp
110.981	6	86.0 x 78.8		2,746	9.0:1	185	6,000	280E	W114	Mar 1972	
110.981	6	86.0 x 78.8		2,746	9.0:1	185	6,000	280CE	W114	Apr 1972	
110.982	6	86.0 x 78.8		2,746	9.0:1	185	6,000	280SL/SLC	W107	Sep 1974	
110.983	6	86.0 x 78.8		2,746	8.7:1	177	6,000	280SEL	W123	Jan 1974	
110.983	6	86.0 x 78.8		2,746	8.7:1	177	6,000	280SE	W116	Aug 1972	
110.984	6	86.0 x 78.8		2,746	8.7:1	177	6,000	280E	W123	Jan 1976	
110.991	6	86.0 x 78.8		2,746	8.0:1	170	6,000	280E	W114	Mar 1972	lo comp
110.991	6	86.0 x 78.8		2,746	8.0:1	170	6,000	280CE	W114	Apr 1972	lo comp
110.992	6	86.0 x 78.8		2,746	8.0:1	170	6,000	280SL/SLC	W107	Sep 1974 to Jul 1975	lo comp
110.993	6	86.0 x 78.8		2,746	8.0:1	170	6,000	280SEL	W116	Jan 1974	lo comp
110.993	6	86.0 x 78.8		2,746	8.0:1	170	6,000	280SE	W116	Aug 1972	lo comp
117.981	8-V	92.0 x 85.0		4,520	8.0:1	195	5,800	300SEL 4.5	W109	Apr 1971 to Oct 1972	
117.982	8-V	92.0 x 85.0		4,520	8.8:1	225	5,000	450SL/SLC	W107	Mar 1973 to Oct 1975	
117.983	8-V	92.0 x 85.0		4,520	8.8:1	225	5,000	450SE	W116	Nov 1972 to Oct 1975	
117.983	8-V	92.0 x 85.0		4,520	8.8:1	225	5,000	450SEL	W116	Mar 1973 to Oct 1975	
117.984	8-V	92.0 x 85.0		4,520	8.0:1	195	5,800	280SE/SEL 4.5	W108	Apr 1971 to Nov 1972	
117.985	8-V	92.0 x 85.0		4,520	8.8:1	217	5,000	450SL/SLC	W107	Oct 1975	K-Jet
117.986	8-V	92.0 x 85.0		4,520	8.8:1	217	5,000	450SE/SEL	W116	Oct 1975	K-Jet
117.992	8-V	92.0 x 85.0		4,520	7.5:1	210	4,800	450SL/SLC	W107	Mar 1972 to Oct 1975	lo comp
117.993	8-V	92.0 x 85.0		4,520	7.5:1	210	4,800	450SE/SEL	W116	Nov 1972 to Oct 1975	lo comp
100.980	8-V	103.0 x 95.0		6,332	8.8:1	250	4,000	600	W100	Jan 1964	
100.981	8-V	103.0 x 95.0		6,332	8.8:1	250	4,000	300SEL 6.3	W109	Dec 1967 to Aug 1972	
100.982	8-V	103.0 x 95.0		6,332	7.3:1	220	4,000	600	W100	Jan 1964	lo comp
100.983	8-V	103.0 x 95.0		6,332	7.3:1	220	4,000	300SEL 6.3	W109	Dec 1967 to Aug 1972	lo comp
100.985	8-V	107.0 x 95.0		6,834	8.8:1	286	4,250	450SEL 6.9	W116	Jun 1975	

The body and assembly plant at Sindelfingen

The Daimler-Benz factory at Untertürkheim